INTERSEX IDENTITY

An Ethical Perspective

Dr. Rekha Ojha

AKANSHA PUBLISHING HOUSE
NEW DELHI • GUWAHATI • VISAKHAPATNAM

AKANSHA PUBLISHING HOUSE
4649-B/21, Ansari Road
Daryaganj, New Delhi-110002
Phones: 23268193, 09435116718
Email: ektabooks@yahoo.com
visit us: www.akanshapublishinghouse.com

Intersex Identity: An Ethical Perspective

First Published 2011

ISBN 978-81-8370-289-8

PRINTED IN INDIA

Published by Akansha Publishing House, New Delhi-110002 and printed at Harmain Offset Press, Delhi.

My Son Parash

Contents

Acknowledgements

"Intersex Identity: An Ethical Perspective" is a research work which highlight the social and philosophical issue related with people born with reproductive or sexual anomaly that does not seem to fit the typical definition of female or male. The book highlight the various social, medical and scientific opinions and theories about what constitutes sex and what constitutes gender. This is not to say that no progress has been made; on the contrary, much has been advanced. But the gaps that still remain be a critical at some of the reasons behind them. That is how this topic came to be decided upon.

As such, I am extremely grateful to all who helped me complete the research and prepare the final output for publication. I am deeply indebted to my husband, Pranesh Roy, who constantly and efficiently prodded me to complete the work upto the stage of preparing this manuscript for publication. I also would like to acknowledge my little son Parash, who unhappily missed me when I was busily involved in research. Finally, my thanks goes to Pradip Debnath who efficiently typeset and proofread my manuscript.

Last but not least, I am deeply beholden to Mr. M.P. Misra, Akansha Publishing House, New Delhi for undertaking publication of this work.

Dr. Rekha Oiha

1

Introduction

"Intersex" is defined as a condition in which there is difficulty in assigning sex to an individual from the appearance of external genitalia. In general term "Intersex" is used for a variety of conditions in which a person is born with a reproductive or sexual anamaly that doesnot seem to fit the typical definition of female or male. In other words we can say that Intersex in humans refers to intermediate or a typical combination of physical features that usually distinguish female from male. This is usually understood to be congenital, involving chromosomal. Morphologic, genital and/or Gonadal anomalies, such as diversion from typical xx-female or xy-male presentations, e.g. sex reversal (xy – female, xx- male), genital ambiguity sex developmental differences. An Intersex individual may have biological characteristics of both the male and the female sexes.[1] Though we speak of Intersex as an inborn condition, Intersex anatomy does not always show up at birth. Sometime a person is not found of Intersex anatomy until she or he reaches the age of puberty, or finds himself an infertile adult, or dies of old age and is autopsied. Some people live and die with Intersex anatomy without anyone (including themselves) ever knowing.

"Intersex" is a general term used for any form of congenital (inborn) mixed sex anatomy. This does not mean that a person with an Intersex condition has all the parts of a male; that is physiologically impossible. What it does mean is that a person with an Intersex condition has some parts usually associated with females, or that she or he has some part that appear ambiguous. It's important to understand that Intersex does not always involve "ambiguous" or blended external sex anatomy sometimes a child or adult who is intersexed can look quite unambiguous sexually, although internally their sex anatomy is mixed. This happen, for example, with complete androgen, insensitivity syndrome, where a person has some male parts (including a y chromosome and lastes) internally, but is quite clear femine on the outside. It's important to also be clear that Intersex is different from transgender in that a person with Intersex is born with mixed sex anatomy, where as a person who is transgendered is a person who feel himself to be a gender different than the one he or she who assigned at birth.

The terms "Third Gender" and "Third sex" describe individuals who are considered to be neither women or men, as well as the social category present in those societies who recognize three or more genders. To different culture or individuals, a third sex or gender may represent an intermediate state between men and women, a state of being both (such as "the spirit of a man in the body of a woman"), the state of being neither (neuter), the ability to cross or swap genders, or another category altogether independent of male and female. The term has been used to describe Hijras of India and Pakistan,[2] Fa'afafine of Polynesia, and Sworn virgins of the Balkans[3] among others, and is also used by many of such groups and individuals to describe themselves. The term "Third" is usually understood to mean "other", some anthropologists and sociologists have described fourth[4], fifth[5] and many[6] genders.

References to a third sex can be found throughout the various texts of India's three ancient spiritual traditions — Hinduism,[7] Jainism[8] and Buddhism[9] — and it can be inferred that Vedic culture recognized three genders. The Vedas (c. 1500 BC - 500 BC) describe individuals as belonging to one of three separate categories, according to one's nature or prakriti. These are also spelled out in the *Kama Sutra* (c. 4th century AD) and elsewhere as *pums-prakriti* (male-nature), *stri-prakriti* (female-nature), and *tritiya-prakriti* (third-nature).[10] Various texts suggest that third sex individuals were well known in pre-modern India, and included male-bodied or female-bodied[11] people as well as intersexuals, and that they can often be recognized from childhood.

The third sex is also discussed in ancient Hindu law, medicine, linguistics and astrology. The foundational work of Hindu law, the *Manusmriti* (c. 200 BC - 200 AD) explains the biological origins of the three sexes: "A male child is produced by a greater quantity of male seed, a female child by the prevalence of the female; if both are equal, a third-sex child or boy and girl twins are produced; if either are weak or deficient in quantity, a failure of conception results."[12] Indian linguist Patanjali's work on Sanskrit grammar, the *Mahabhasya* (c. 200 BC), states that Sanskrit's three grammatical genders are derived from three natural genders. The earliest Tamil grammar, the Tolkappiyam (3rd century BC) also refers to hermaphrodites as a third "neuter" gender (in addition to a feminine category of unmasculine males). In Vedic astrology, the nine planets are each assigned to one of the three genders; the third gender, *tritiya-prakriti*, is associated with Mercury, Saturn and (in particular) Ketu. In the Puranas, there are also references to three kinds of devas of music and dance: apsaras (female), gandharvas (male) and kinnars (neuter).

The two great Sanskrit epic poems, the *Ramayana* and the *Mahabharata*,[13] also indicate the existence of a third gender in ancient Indic society. Some versions of *Ramayana* tell that in one part of the story, the hero Rama heads into exile in the forest. Halfway there, he discovers that most of the people of his home town Ayodhya were following him. He told them, "Men and women, turn back," and with that, those who were "neither men nor women" did not know what to do, so they stayed there. When Rama returned from exile years later, he discovered them still there and blessed them, saying that there will be a day when they will rule the world.

In the Buddhist *Vinaya*, codified in its present form around the 2nd century BC and said to be handed down by oral tradition from Buddha himself, there are four main sex/gender categories:

males, females, *ubhatobyanjanaka* (people of a dual sexual nature) and *pandaka* (people of various non-normative sexual natures, perhaps originally denoting a deficiency in male sexual capacity).[14] As the *Vinaya* tradition developed, the term *pandaka* came to refer to a broad third sex category which encompassed intersex, male and female bodied people with physical and/or behavioural attributes that were considered inconsistent with the sexual ideal of man and woman.[15]

In many countries around the world, there are no early surgeries to "treat" intersex bodies. These people's main issues are often based on not being able to fit into either gender or growing up with a body incompatible with the gender in which they were raised. The very theories used to support mutilating intersex bodies both surgically and hormonally are based on notions of gender which have been proved to be unreliable. According to the theories often espoused by followers of Dr. John Money. Gender is not innate to the individual. We have no proof of this. We do have quite a bit of proof to the contrary.

Intersex is not just about our bodies but also about how we perceive ourselves within those bodies and gender identity is a crucial part of everyone's identity. In most societies, intersex individuals do end up living in one gender role or the other and have either a male or female gender identity.

The aim of this book is to propose a plausible conceptual framework, which actually carries relevance in various fields of application for the concept of equality in human and gender, especially third gender rights discourses. My particular emphasis will be to see full human rights for all people born with intersex conditions and also of those rights should be the right to self identity. They should have all rights granted all other people.

In any society we understand intersexuality primarily as an issue of stigma and emotional trauma. In our culture, sexual variation which blurs the line between male and female is stigmatized. Intersexuality is so highly stigmatized that, until recently, the phenomenon was little known outside related medical specialties. Thus, the birth of an intersex child is emotionally traumatizing. Parents are traumatized because the birth of a child with sexual ambiguity violets a deeply held world view, and because it elicits parental feelings and shame and guilty. The parents are traumatized because of the general belief that Hijras are a distinct group of people, they have malformed genitalia. It is believed that if the Hijras get to know the child has ambiguous genitalia they will take away the child. Parents are afraid/confused/ashamed to talk about the problem of their child and seek help. But they simply don't understand that the problem is not their child but it is the society as a whole produces such problems. They must understand that the constitution guarantees to every person the fundamental right not to be denied by the state, equality before the law or the equal protection of laws within the territory of India (article 14). It prohibits the state to discriminate against any citizen on ground only of religion, race, caste, 'sex', place of birth or any of them. The problem which I am going to highlight is regarding the special protection and preferential treatment in favour of Hijras. The reason of their low status, illiteracy, economic dependence, social restrictions, religious prohibitions and overall apathetic and callous attitudes of the people and society.

I have come to this topic (The third sex: An Identity Issue) as an ethical philosopher. My initial interest was actually in dealing with these philosophical questions related to Intersex or Hijras, which are given below:

- What is biological sex?
- What is it to be male or female or both or both not?
- Does biological sex exist at all independently of our beliefs about sex or gender?
- How do norms of masculinity and femininity affect scientific understanding of sex?
- What can intersex , transsex and transgender teach us about the nature of sex?
- Could and should we abandon the practice of classifying one another by sex?

- What is gender? Is gender mental or bodily, or is this a false opposition? Does gender exist only to the extent that we perform it?
- Should the concept of gender be replaced or supplemented by the concept of the imaginary body?
- What is the relationship between gender inequality and the injustices that gays and lesbians suffer?
- Are their sexual practices that should be avoided (or promoted) because they are connected to (or free from) gender and other equalities?
- Can we understand sexuality as shaped by gender relation, or must sexuality be understood in terms of a theory of 'sexual difference' and not a theory of gender etc?

Socially constructed role prevent Intersex people from realizing their true potential, deny them information, education, and health care, rob them of the power to make decisions, make them susceptible to violence, abuse and exploitation, take away their right and to earn a living and deprive them of legal protection. This being the fact sheet, what needs to be done is to level the playing field for intersexual people. Here comes again the relevance and urgency of the concept of equality in practice.

I hope my study will make important contribution to the global efforts to recognize Intersex rights as human rights. Human rights are the basic rights and freedoms to which all humans are entitled, often held to include the right to life and liberty, freedom of though and expression, and equality before the law. Here, a substantive conception of equality is called for in order to bring about in a possible future a formal consideration of equality for all humans. Only when the playing field is equal can equality for all humans be formalized. This is the crux of the present study.

NOTES & REFERENCES

1. "Online Glossary of Technical Terms in plant Pathology"" Plantpathcornell.edu, http://www.plantpath.cornell.edu/glossary/defsI.htm retrieved 2009-08-21)

2. Agarwal, Anuja (1997), *Gendered Bodies: the Case of the 'Third Gender' in India*, Contributions to Indian Sociology, n.s., 31 (1997): 273-97
3. Young, Will (2000), *Women Who Become Men: Albanian Sworn Virgins*. ISBN 1-85973-335-2
4. Roscoe, Will (2000). *Changing Ones: Third and Fourth Genders in Native North America*. Palgrave Macmillan (June 17, 2000); See also: Trumbach, Randolph (1994). *London's Sapphists: From Three Sexes to Four Genders in the Making of Modern Culture*. In Gilbert Herdt, (ed.) *Third Sex, Third Gender: Beyond Sexual Dimorphism in Culture and History*, 111-36. New York: Zone (MIT).
5. Graham, Sharyn (2001), Sulawesi's fifth gender, *Inside Indonesia*, April-June 2001.
6. Martin, M. Kay and Voorhies, Barbara (1975). *Supernumerary Sexes*, chapter 4 of Female of the Species (New York: Columbia University Press, 1975), 23.
7. Wilhelm, Amara Das (2004). *Tritiya Prakriti (People of the Third Sex): Understanding Homosexuality, Transgender Identity and Intersex Conditions through Hinduism* (XLibris Corporation, 2004).
8. Zwilling, Leonard and Sweet, Michael (1996). Like a City Ablaze: The Third Sex and the Creation of Sexuality in Jain Religious Literature, *Journal of the History of Sexuality*, 6 (3), pp.359-384.
9. Jackson, Peter A. (1996). Non-normative Sex/Gender Categories in the Theravada Buddhist Scriptures, *Australian Humanities Review*, April 1996.
10. Alternate transliteration: trihytiya prakrihyti
11. Historian Walter Penrose wrote that "distinct social and economic roles once existed for women thought to belong to a third gender. Hidden in history, these women dressed in men's clothing, served as porters and personal bodyguards to kings and queens, and even took an active role in sex with women." Penrose, Walter (2001). Hidden in History: Female Homoeroticism and Women of a Third Nature in the South Asian Past, *Journal of the History of Sexuality* 10.1 (2001), p. 4
12. *Manusmriti*, 3.49. Text online
13. The hero Arjuna takes a "vow of eunuchism" to live as the third sex for a year: "O lord of the Earth, I will declare myself as one of

the neuter sex. O monarch, it is, indeed difficult to hide the marks of the bowstring on my arms. I will, however, cover both my cicatrized arms with bangles. Wearing brilliant rings on my ears and conch-bangles on my wrists and causing a braid to hang down from my head, I shall, O king, appear as one of the third sex, Vrihannala by name. And living as a female I shall (always) entertain the king and the inmates of the inner apartments by reciting stories. And, O king, I shall also instruct the women of Virata's palace in singing and delightful modes of dancing and in musical instruments of diverse kinds. And I shall also recite the various excellent acts of men... ." *Mahabharata* (Virata-parva), Translated by Ganguli, Kisari Mohan. Project Gutenberg.

14. Jackson, Peter A. (1996). *Ibid.*
15. Gyatso, Janet (2003). One Plus One Makes Three: Buddhist Gender Conceptions and the Law of the Non-Excluded Middle, *History of Religions*. 2003, no. 2. University of Chicago Press.

2

Intersex Issue: Literature Review

The available literature in Intersex issue are mainly consists of books, reports of studies, conferences and workshops conducted by international and domestic government and non-government organizations (NGOs). The recent importance accorded to Intersex on the international agenda is responsible for the rise in the number of ongoing research studies on Intersex.

Lessons from the Intersexed: A landmark work on gender theory and activism written by Sozanne J. Kessler. This is an excellent book on the "gender theory". It is also a starting point for new gender activism. Kessler tells us the intersexed "real lives stories" of pain and suffering. She deconstructs the medical rhetoric as to how doctors "enforce gender" while inflicting both physical and psychic harm on their intersexed patients. She compares the genital reconstruction imposed on the intersexed with that begrudgingly provided to (m-to-f) transsexual women and suggested to women with genital cancer. Kessler shows a how we might change gender for the benefit of all. She says, "Institutionalized mutilations occur because the genitals too are taken too seriously....If we want people to respect particular bodies, they need to be taught to lose respect for ideal ones." She suggests that genital piercing, people creating "custom" genitals or men growing breast for their own self-pleasure are initial steps to breaking down the connation between body and gender. From that the two gender system will break down.

Her book has a large number of foot notes and cross references to other works. She is well read and very current. The text is some 131 pages. The footnotes are another 30 pages.

The glossary is 4 pages. The bibliography is 10 pages. And the index is another 12. This a very well researched book with innovative ideas.

Her closing words are: "We must use whatever means to we have to give up on gender. The problems of intersexuality [and gayness, transsexuals, transivities, etc.] will vanish and we will, compensate intersexuals for all the lessons they have provided."

Fixing Sex: Intersex, Medical Authority, and Lived Experience: A much needed addition to literature on Intersex. Katrina Karkazis' *Fixing Sex* is an ambitious attempt to deal with the multiple issues brought up by those born with Intersex Conditions (I'm going to use that term over DSDs) their parents and the doctors who 'treated' them. She comes clearly down on the side against performing 'normalising' procedures on infants often by performing surgery on larger than average clitorises (in some cases, performing actual clitorodectomies) or reassigning xy children with micropenises as female. She points out how doctors are slowly reevaluating how these procedures are done (or whether they're done) but are still highly defensive about the medical decisions they're made and, especially, about the harm they've caused.

For those following the Intersex community and their often heartbreaking stories, the book can be painful to read. But Ms. Karkazis tries to present the material not as an advocate, but as a medical ethicist and she succeeds brilliantly in shining much light on a lot of dark histories than are still threatening to all involved. It's in dealing with these bioethical questions the book finds its greatest success. She balances the choices parents and doctors made for infants with the anger and helplessness of those children who had to actually live with those decisions. She also points out how adherence to 'normality' and the gender binary had everything to do with many of these (often for the worse) life-altering decisions.

There are some parts of the discussion I wished the book had keyed into with more detail and first person narratives. She talks to almost no one who was gender reassigned, either those still living in their assigned gender nor those who were uncomfortable in their assigned gender and later transitioned back. I feel she shortchanges some of the connections between the Intersex and Trans-communities, which includes a goodly number of people born with Intersex conditions. Perhaps it's Karkazis seeming connections to Bo Laurent (formerly Cheryl Chase) and Alice Dreger that kept her from discussing this important linkage between the two communities. I was also disturbed that Karkazis, in a discussion of David Reimer and gender identity, makes a fairly sweeping conclusion about in utero hormonal exposure, and CAH (and I don't think anyone would say exposure to hormones is the same for anyone, there are many biological and experiential factors that can alter the outcome) that I found myself shaking my head while reading.

Likewise, she makes a statement that David Reimer was one case, but there was another similar non-Intersex reassignment case where the reassignment worked and that, somehow modifies the conclusions of Milton Diamond and William Reiner and others. However, she gives information in her endnotes that suggests this reassignment might not have worked quite as well as how she referenced it in the main body of her text. It was a little sloppy.

Still, anyone interested in Intersex, bioethics, gender and just the intense human drama that surrounds how we 'normalize' sex and gender owes it to themselves to read Fixing Sex. The many anonymous quotes in the book and still-raging debates between defensive medical practitioners, angry Intersex adults, guilt-ridden parents and dueling support organizations show how painful an issue this is, and Karkazis has done a wonderful navigating through it.

Fixing Sex is the best book I have ever read over the years which deals with the ethical issues which have plagued the intersex community, parents and doctors. One reason is that it is meticulously researched and in the introduction, the author helps the reader understand her methodology and also makes it transparent and easy to grasp for the reader who is not familiar with such research.

The author is also very accurate about the medical aspects of various intersex conditions (something that often was not true with previous books by researchers dealing with the ethical debate, unfortunately.) However, the main reason I feel the book is a success is that is shows respect for ALL stakeholders, something which has thus far not been the case and this will help in the future I hope in such a way that not just the parents and doctors will be able to have a dialog, but actual intersex adults also will be more likely to be included.

She has done something that is very difficult to do. Katrina Karkazis has written a book that both I (an intersex activist) and a medical doctor can read and understand and not be upset about. Now that is a tour de force.

Myths of Gender: Biological Theories About Women And Men, Revised Edition: by Anne Fausto-Sterling This book is a gem among the gender rubble. I'm not surprised that more people haven't read this book, because it gives the human being a maze of possibilities and HUMAN potential not limited by gender, which maybe to frightening for the Mars and Venuses public to accept, since it leaves the door wide open for limitless potential and variations among persons attributed to individuality and not gender. I found other gender related books to be very limiting, which lead me to take some tests on spatial and verbal ability, let's just say, under the narrow Brain Sex mode, I would have a completely male brain in a female body!.. after my test, my suspicions increased and I did some further reading and found this book. The writer explains how researchers may not be entirely objective, how you cannot in any way base all gender behavior on a limited amount of subjects, since we of course have over a billion persons roaming the planet with many different individual abilities, and how there is an agenda against women's advancement in science and math, which of course demand sound logic and spatial reasoning. Expand your possibilities, get the gender limits off your minds, and soar!

I was always puzzled when it came to these gender studies. Anee Fausto Sterling tells us about how these studies are subjective and misleading. How and why we find a continual staple of books proclaiming 'innate sex differences". From my own experiences, none of the sex difference books hold water when it comes to the reality of everyday life. We see such differences in individuals as to say it's not sex which is the cause behind them. Everyone should read her book. It is time to stop reinforcing sterotypes on people.

Anne Fausto-Sterling attempts to discredit a variety of studies purporting to show fixed biological differences between the sexes. She is not completely successful. It is obvious that plenty of what has been believed about human females has proved false with time but for me A F-S goes a little too far in the opposite direction. Much of the nature/nurture argument is impossible to prove either way and the input of both is probably more equal than A F-S will allow.

Some of her arguments are also weak or wrong such as her suggestion that Santo Domingo 'penis at twelve' people actually have a choice in 'becoming' male or that in some cultures males do the bulk of the childcare. She does, though, provide an important amount of exposure of conflicting evidence across many studies from verbal skills, math, spatial ability to brain differences and hormones.

An important point she makes is about how we choose to understand difference and what we want to do about it. We all know that if some difference is supposedly found in males then this will automatically be given high status regardless of what that difference is. This is what is at the root of much of the argument of this book and at the root of women trying to destroy difference. But it would be strange if evolution has not selected for different bodies and behaviors to better suit the different ways men and women have been able to achieve reproductive success. It is important not to avoid the biology just to avoid male bias and what male dominated culture has been able to impose in the past.

I read it before I read "Brain Sex" so I wasn't at all able to be programmed into a set of beliefs so common these days.

Gender studies are flawed, they involve the subjectivity of the "researcher" and bias. If the "researcher finds a woman to have a road map and blueprints in her mind, she's said to have been exposed to male hormones, as though a woman cannot have these gifts without being somehow a "misfit" according to most "researchers". And what of the man who has great writing and memory but poor spatial and math ability? He is neatly fitted into a category of male who was exposed to female hormones. Anyway the writer debunks these myths with straightforward writing and objective conclusions to confusing answers other writers come up with to explain a man with a female brain and a woman with a male brain. The "researchers" have assigned a very narrow set of abilities to males and females, and they use the hormone theory to perpetuate it. Hormones are cousins, and estrogen, androgens, testosterone, progesterone are found in both sexes and in individual amounts. This in turn gives little truth to the notion of hormones playing a part in male or female brain wiring. Brains are not fixed, a spatial brain can be in a female and a verbal in a male.

Same Difference: How Gender Myths Are Hurting Our Relationships, Our Children, and Our Jobs by Rosalind Barnett and Caryl Rivers : I read this book with some eagerness. However, I ended up feeling rather disappointed and concluding that—while it makes some good points—it suffers from many of the same criticisms it points out in the work of feminist scholars.

As an example, the book devotes an inordinate amount of space to criticizing the work of Carol Gilligan. I was actually glad to see this, because the authors correctly point out that Gilligan's work has had a disproportionate and scary amount of influence on cultural thought despite severe methodological flaws (e.g., small sample, reliance on unrepresentative anecdotal accounts, refusal to allow other researchers access to data, etc.). However—and without any apparent sense of irony—Barnett and Rivers rely heavily on anecdotes from their own clinical practices throughout the book to make THEIR points. And if it's not okay for Gilligan to do so, why is it okay for them?

A second feature I found disappointing in this book is that the authors misinterpret "small differences" to mean trivial or meaningless. For example, a frequent refrain throughout the book is that studies comparing genders find more variability within genders than between genders. This is undoubtedly true, but it does not mean that the obtained mean differences are unimportant. As an illustration, take the height difference in men and women. Few people would argue that men, on average, are taller than women. Of course, there is greater variability within genders than between; in other words, the difference between the tallest ten percent of men and shortest ten percent is greater than the difference between the average man and woman. But that does not call into question the documented sex difference: Men are, on average, taller than women, and this difference reflects innate biological sex differences. Height, of course, is a trivial trait I chose to make the point vividly, but the same argument can be made about any of the cognitive and psychological traits that solid science (e.g., peer-reviewed meta-analyses) reveals to demonstrate sex differences. To give a more substantive example, while men and women do not differ on overall IQ, they DO differ in the shape of the distribution, with men being disproportionately represented in the tails. To put it bluntly, there are more severely retarded men...but there are also more male geniuses. Why, nobody knows, but it does no good to try to pretend these differences don't exist or to blame it on some nonexistent glass ceiling that is preventing women from geniushood.

In short, I feel this book goes too far in trying to deny the existence of sex differences. I agree with the authors that the "Men are from Mars" and Carol Gilligan crowd is doing a disservice to men and women alike by stereotyping and pigeonholing us and insisting that we do not have the capabilities or flexibilities to show traits associated with the opposite gender. But I think "Same Difference" undermines their own argument by insisting too steadfastly that there are no differences at all, and their argument is undermined further by a willingness to rely on anecdotal evidence they (rightfully) dismiss in others' work. Yes, there is tremendous variability within genders, and both men and women are capable of an infinite range of behaviors, emotions, and talents. But men and women also differ, reliably, consistently, and in statistically significant and practically important ways. To pretend that they don't is the tale of the emperor's new clothes all over again.

Intersex and Identity: The Contested Self by Sharon E. Preves: I highly recommend this book for anyone wanting to learn what intersex means and what it means to be intersexed. The stories are heart breaking and heart warming all at the same time. I found myself experiencing a wide range of emotions from the deepest sense of compassion to outright rage at the medical community and the closed-minded behaviors of parents and families. There is so little known about this subject that the behavior of physicians and families isn't really all that surprising but it is still maddening! This book helped demystify the topic and make it a very real "condition" that needs much more than a biological definition and diagnosis.

Bodies in Doubt: An American History of Intersex by Elizabeth Reis: What does it mean to be human? Humanity incorporates physical and cultural sexuality - yet not all bodies are clearly male or female. BODIES IN DOUBT: AN AMERICAN HISTORY OF INTERSEX offers a historical, cultural, social and medical survey of intersex in America from early to modern times and argues that medical practice cannot exist outside of broader cultural influences. This history of how Americans have handled ambiguous bodies and changing criteria for judging proves it - and is key to any health collection.

Intersex in the Age of Ethics (Ethics in Clinical Medicine Series) by Alice Domurat Dreger: Alice Domurat Dreger has written what may well come to be regarded as the definitive work on intersexuality. By employing a collective and inclusive approach, Ms. Dreger is able to provide both personal and medical perspectives on intersexuality provided by individuals, their families and compassionate medical providers. She provides a brief forward to each chapter on the author and topic content which is illuminating and helps to assist the reader to focus on the material. This is a well-written book which, for the first time in a single printed volume, provides material solely dealing with intersexed individuals. This landmark book provides compelling reasons, based on the telling of personal odysseys, why only those people affected should be the decision makers in their care. I hope that every intersexed person, every family member or parent of an intersexed individual reads this book. And I pray that every medical professional who treats intersexed individuals, beginning with obstetricians, pediatricians and pediatric urologists, takes to heart the suggestions for adapting care to a patient-directed philosophy of medical care.

In her most recent book, *Sexing the Body: Gender Politics and the Construction of Sexuality* (Fausto-Sterling, 2000), Fausto-Sterling maintains that human sexuality is best understood not as a dichotomy but as a continuum. She bases this assertion on her beliefs regarding intersex conditions. A chapter subtitled "The Sexual Continuum" begins with the case of Levi Suydam, an intersexual living in the 1840s who menstruated regularly but who also had a penis and testicles. Fausto-Sterling writes:

> While male and female stand on the extreme ends of a biological continuum, there are many bodies, bodies such as Suydam's, that evidently mix together anatomical components conventionally attributed to both males and females. The implications of my argument for a sexual continuum are profound. If nature really offers us more than two sexes, then it follows that our current notions of masculinity and femininity are cultural conceits.
>
> ... Modern surgical techniques help maintain the two-sex system. Today children who are born "either/or-neither/both"—a fairly common phenomenon—usually disappear from view because doctors "correct" them right away with surgery. (Fausto-Sterling, 2000, p. 31)

Since 1990, when Suzanne Kessler published her

foundational feminist critique of the modern-day medical treatment of children with intersex, much has changed in intersex politics, practice, and theory. This essay traces some key points of progress and considers in particular the relationship of academic feminism and intersex advocacy; proof of and reasons for success in intersex medical advocacy; and intersex identity politics, especially with regard to the nature-nurture debate and terminology (intersex versus hermaphroditism versus disorders of sex development). The authors are university-based academic feminists who have worked intensively as volunteers and as paid directors at the Intersex Society of North America, the longest-running and best-known intersex advocacy and policy organization. In this work, they draw on the published literature as well as their own activist and academic experiences. They argue that, in the last fifteen years, much progress has been made in terms of improving the medical and social attitudes toward people with intersex, but that significant work remains to be done to ensure that children born with sex anomalies will be treated in a way that privileges their long-term well-being over societal norms. They also argue that, while feminist scholars have been critically important in developing the theoretical underpinnings of the intersex rights movement and sometimes in carrying out the day-to-day political work of that movement, there have been intellectual and political problems with some feminists' approaches to intersex.

The Truth about Me by A. Revati: This book is a text symptomatic of our times. From the title, the book makes a claim on something definitive called the 'truth' and a fixed identity called 'me.' In the Preface, Revathy, the author makes her ambitions for the book clear. Her earlier edited book Unarvum Uruvamum, a collection of hijra life stories helped achieve a lot in Tamil Nadu, the only state where a separate category of voter registration for aravanis or hijras exists) and Revathy hopes this book will achieve more. She tells us she will tell us of her 'innermost life' and that she hopes to show that hijras are capable of more than begging and sex work (as if these are not difficult enough!) and in what will be the first of several rehearsed clichés, that she does not seek sympathy but hijra rights.

The symptoms which Revathy's book embodies are a) the publishing project that makes of a life a project. It is difficult to call this autobiography because it is not the writing of a life impelled by internal drives to reflect upon a life but as a project for subaltern visibility and middle class voyeurism and b) the NGOised individual whose life is flattened out by the rhetoric of identity speak and right speak, the language demanded by the aforementioned project.

Revathy's prose is flat and monochromatic and this is worsened by the regular eruptions of right speak in it. The narrative is linear and prosaic, the translation pedestrian and awkward (idiomatically wrong English, mistakes, proofing errors). Far from the innermost life, most of the narrative is exteriorised and runs along a teleological path. There's little or no space for contradiction, dilemma, doubt (surely founding elements of all our psyches), let alone self-reflexivity and self-critique.

If you are looking for a narrative of almost unadulterated victimhood (the moments of relief are few and far between), an elaborate insider's look into the rituals and anthropology of hijra life, the difficulties of a sex worker's life, especially harassment from the police (and here is where the voyeurism creeps in inevitably, apart from the problem in asking the hijra to evoke these narratives repeatedly in an NGOised context) and so on, then you will not be disappointed.

There are also genuine and poignant moments of bonding, violence and endurance in the narrative. But what is missing is any worthwhile reflection on all this. There are so many moments of productive social contradiction, of irony, none of which are explored. The fact that the family's hijra child is the only child who really cares about the parents and the family as a whole even as she is abused all her life in its spaces for being a hijra and the fact that Revathy's NGOisation alienates her from the hijra community rendering her unable to go back and forcing her to return to the NGO, to offer just two examples of the possibility for some thinking and writing that might have pushed Revathy and us as readers into interesting insights about ourselves and help us develop perspective on some of the more intractable contradictions in how we construct ourselves as political subjects.

That Revathy is not self-righteous and that her tone tends to be dispassionate are boons but she seems cowed down by the need to be spokesperson, representative and this leaves no room for any real exploration into what constitutes Revathy's 'innermost life.' She starts her narrative at the beginning and ends where she is now. Instead, if she had begun medias as, shown us how she felt about a particular moment in all its constitutive complexity, we might have had a powerful narrative.

Instead, we have a rushed, exterior, seamless narrative of continuity with some ups and several more downs that do not give us the fullness of experience. The productive moments end abruptly as the narrative marches on, making it difficult for the reader to even have the space to mull over a moment as it is textually truncated and the space for it can be only extra-textual which is the not the hallmark of good autobiographical writing. Revathy might have worked with a better editor, a co-author or indeed just spent more time thinking about her life for us to have truly benefited from it.

With Respect to Sex: Negotiating Hijra Identity in South India (Worlds of Desire: The Chicago Series on Sexuality, Gender, and Culture) by Gayatri Reddy: I had to read this for class. It was a mostly painful experience of thinking abstractly about the "third gender." As far as gender studies go, which I have very little interest on the academic level, I can image worse books. This book at least has narrative portions. Excluding chapter 1 it is actually readable. The idea of respect or "izzat" as being a primary consideration animating life for the Hijra is interesting. But as far as the foundations of Reddy's ideas, it's mostly the post-modern babble students today are used to.... ie gender is an essentially unknowable matter of performance and desire rather than a unchangeable reality of the self.

AIDS Sutra: Untold Stories from India by Amartya Sen: AIDS has been known in India since the 1980s. In the ensuing decades, numerous alarms have been rung, but with a few exceptions the government, health establishment, and even the constantly vaunted new middle class have perpetuated misinformation, practiced outrageous discrimination, and made little effort to offer effective treatment or prevention to the millions of people affected by or at risk of the virus (estimates for the number of people currently infected in India range from 2 to 5 million). This anthology of new essays by the literary and journalistic elite of India is intended to raise consciousness. Aside from economist Amartya Sen's foreword, which speculates about economic effects and the question of personal responsibility, the essays are all personal stories that, despite the inclusion of famous authors (including Salman Rushdie), have no distinctive literary merit. The intent to counter the belief that AIDS happens to "other people" is weakened by the fact that most of the essays describe marginal or oppressed people who will seem exotic to middle-class readers.

Third Sex, Third Gender: Beyond Sexual Dimorphism in Culture and History by Gilbert Herdt (ed.): Bringing together historical and anthropological studies, Third Sex, Third Gender challenges the usual emphasis on sexual dimorphism an reproduction, providing a unique perspective on the various forms of socialization of people who are neither "male" nor "female." The existence of a third sex or gender enables us to understand how Byzantine palace eunuchs and Indian hijras met the criteria of special social roles that necessitated practices such as self-castration, and how intimate the forbidden desires were expressed among the Dutch Sodomites in the early modern period, the Sapphists of eighteenth-century England or the so-called hermaphrodite-homosexuals of nineteenth-century Europe and America. By contextualizing these practices and by allowing these bodies, meanings and desires to emerge, *Third Sex, Third Gender* provides a new way to think about sex and gender systems that is crucial to contemporary debates within the social sciences.

"This book introduces a significantly new dimension into current debates on gender and sexuality. An impressive range of cross-cultural materials, from historical and contemporary societies, comments on the way the 'third term' can become an end in itself. Where sex is not tied to reproduction alone nor gender only to dualistic thinking, 'third' possibilities emerge in people's social and existential strivings. There is much here to challenge those suppositions - whether taken for granted or the fuel for critique - based on a two-sex gender model. The authors are at once serious and adventurous in their task, and the result in an original, courageous collection."

The Invisibles: A Tale of the Eunuchs of India by Zia Jaffrey: Zia Jaffrey, daughter of the well-known Indian food writer Madhur Jaffrey and heir to a hybrid Indian-American culture, found herself fascinated on a visit to India by a separate and extraordinary caste—the hijras, or eunuchs, castrati who dress as women and live together. Empathizing with their sense of otherness, she pursued the story of their semi-secret existence. The hijras have a long tradition in India, yet are regarded with great ambiguity. On the one hand they are invited to attend weddings and births and thought to bring good luck despite their crude behavior, bawdy jokes, and bad singing. On the other hand, there is much fearful speculation as to how they perpetuate their caste—some allege the abduction and castration of little boys. Freelance writer Jaffrey, an American of Indian extraction, traveled throughout India to study eunuchs, or "hijras." The subculture of castrated males has existed in India for centuries, owing to their outcast status and the tendency of government officials to discourage inquiries, but their living arrangements, social structure and actual numbers are difficult to verify. Jaffrey provides a wealth of previous research, including folklore regarding hijras' activities, as well as details of the interesting but inconclusive interviews she conducted with hijras living in India today. Although those she interviewed acknowledge that they arrive unasked to bring good luck by singing and dancing at weddings and celebrations for newborns, other questions regarding castration ceremonies, prostitution, religious practices and hierarchical organization elicited elusive and contradictory responses.

Gender Diversity: Crosscultural Variations by Serena Nanda: How can we gain new understandings about sex, gender, and sexuality? What are the relationships between culture and gender diversity? How has the diffusion of Euro-American culture affected the sex/gender ideologies of non-European cultures? This eye-opening account of the differences in how sex/gender diversity is experienced in seven cultures raises our consciousness and challenges our intellectual understandings and attitudes about what we consider natural, normal, and morally right. Nanda's examples, which reveal the complexity of social responses toward sex/gender diversity, are ethnographically well documented and represent various geographical areas and sex/gender ideologies. In classic anthropological fashion, Nanda's text enables us to cross the barriers of cultural difference to a recognition of a greater shared humanity.

In this lean book, Serena Nanda uses ethnographic accounts to illustrate how diverse cultures construct their sex/gender systems. By doing so, she reveals that these systems are not always binary; male and female, man and woman. Her descriptions of masculinity and femininity in India, Brazil, Polynesia, Thailand, the Philippines, within some Native American tribes and in contemporary Euro-American cultures challenge what some believe is "natural" about gender and, by extension, sexuality. By presenting gender variations historically and as they are currently understood and displayed, Nanda reveals the social, historical and cultural forces that have created changes in these sex/gender systems.

This engaging book has eight short chapters. The introductory chapter lays the foundation for Nanda's argument by defining key terms (e.g., gender diversity, sex, gender, sexual orientation, transgendered, sex/gender identity, etc.) with which readers must be familiar to understand gender variation. Chapters 1 through 5 provide ethnographic accounts of multiple genders among North American Indians, the hijra and sadhin of India, the travestís, bichas, and viados of Brazil, the mahu in Polynesia, the kathoey of Thailand and the bayot/bantut/bakla in the Philippines. What some readers will find most interesting and provocative are accounts of how contact with Western cultures influenced existing gender constructs in these cultures. For example, North American Indian men who dressed like women, did "women's work" and were sexually intimate with other men were called "berdache" (an Arabic term for a male prostitute) and demeaned by early Spanish explorers on religious grounds.

Chapter 6 focuses on sex and gender diversity in Euro-American cultures. While the present-day view is that there are only two sexes and two genders, Nanda reveals other models of sex/gender that are part of the Euro-American heritage. In the final chapter, Nanda summarizes important ideas from the preceding chapters and compares sex/gender variations. This further exposes the extent to which sex/gender variants challenge the binary concepts of sex, gender and sexuality in Western cultures. She rightly concludes that "the evidence argues against any one-way, cause-and-effect relationship between homosexuality and sex/gender diversity, and a specific sexuality may well emerge from a sex/gender variant role, rather than the reverse...the association between sexuality and sex/gender diversity cannot be assumed, but rather must be examined within specific cultural/historical contexts" (Nanda 2000, 101-02).

For those who want to learn more, Nanda includes a reference section that highlights materials that should be of particular interest to "students" of gender. She also provides a list of selected films, explains how each complements materials presented in a particular chapter and where to obtain the film.

Some readers may be disappointed that there is little coverage of female gender diversity in this book. However, this shortcoming is not Nanda's. As she explains, socialization, patriarchy and other factors allow male gender variance to occur more frequently than female gender variance. To her credit, where female gender variance is well documented (e.g.,among North American Indians, the s dhin of India and Euro-American variations) Nanda provides ample coverage.

In short, this book is a refreshing addition to the literature on gender, sexuality, cultural studies and gay and lesbian studies that should not be overlooked.

Sexing the Body: Gender Politics and the Construction of Sexuality by Anne Fausto-Sterling: Anyone who has been following the new brain science in the popular press—and even those whose casual reading includes journals along the lines of Psychoneuroendocrinology—will be fascinated by the puckish observations of Brown University biologist Anne Fausto-Sterling, whose provocative and erudite essays easily establish the cultural biases underlying current scientific thought on gender. She goes on to critique the science itself, exposing inconsistencies in the literature and weaknesses in the rhetorical and theoretical structures that support new research. "One of the major claims I make in this book," she explains, "is that labeling someone a man or a woman is a social decision. We may use scientific knowledge to help us make the decision, but only our beliefs about gender—not science—can define our sex. Furthermore, our beliefs about gender affect what kinds of knowledge scientists produce about sex in the first place." Whether discussing genital surgery on intersex infants or the amorous lives of lab rats, the author is unfailingly clear and convincing, and manages to impart humor to subjects as seemingly unpromising as neuroanatomy and the structure of proteins. —Regina Marler —This text refers to an out of print or unavailable edition of this title.

As the old complaint that men's long hairstyles make it impossible to tell "if it's a boy or a girl" reveals, gender ambiguity is socially unsettling to many people. Boldly stepping into the breach, Fausto-Sterling contends that the fear of gender confusion has pushed science and medicine to go to extreme lengths in constructing solid concepts of sex (i.e., an individual's anatomical attributes) and gender (i.e., the internal conviction of one's maleness or femaleness). As in her now classic book, Myths of Gender, Fausto-Sterling draws on a wealth of scientific and medical information, along with social, anthropological and feminist theory, to make the case that "choosing which criteria to use in determining sex, and choosing to make the determination at all, are social decisions for which scientists can offer no absolute guidelines." Further, she adds, "our beliefs about gender affect what kind of knowledge scientists produce about sex in the first place." While the book encompasses a wide range of topics—including a cultural history of hermaphroditism (now more properly termed "intersexuality") and the recent medical interventions used to "cure" it, an account of the emergence of sex hormone research and its use to create changes in sexual orientation, and the history of how science has (mis)understood the brain in terms of gender—Fausto-Sterling's cogent use of concrete historical examples, her simple language and personal anecdotes keep this complex synthesis accessible. Her insightful work offers profound challenges to scientific research, the creation of social policy and the future of feminist and gender theory.

The existing literature in Intersex people do not discuss the complexity of the issue. Being a complex phenomenon, Intersex people's problem can be viewed from different perspectives. The problem is deeply rooted in sociocultural reality. Intersex people surrounded in ambiguities involving issues which most would prefer to avoid. The process of clarity will involve numerous debates and arguments. One may say that Intersex problem is in the inception stage, offering an opportunity for all to deeply reflect on their problems and keeping in mind that the Intersex people are most affected.

3

The Social and Philosophical Construction of Sex and Gender

The concept of sex and gender has been the subject of intense debate within feminist philosophy and theory of the past forty years. To follow these debates, we must first deepen our grasp of the initial definition of sex and gender which psychologist and sociologists took up.

'Gender' is social and consist of social expectation and assumption about what behaviours and traits are appropriate for male and female individuals. It is the psychological traits, and the understandings of themselves that individuals tend to develop under the influence of these social expectation. For example, it is commonly expected that males will relish confrontation while female will try to avoid it. On the other hand 'sex' is the condition of being biologically male of female. A human being is biologically male if they have 'xy' chromosomes, testes, 'male' internal and external genitalia, a relatively high proportion of androgens, and 'male' secondary sex characteristics. A human being is biologically female if they have 'xx' chromosomes, ovaries, 'female' internal and external genitalia, relatively high proportion of estrogen and progesterone, and 'female' secondary sex characteristics. One might accuse these definition of being circular, since they say that part of what defines being male) or female) is having 'male' (or 'female') genitalia and secondary characteristics. However 'male' (or 'female') is here are only being used as shorthand for, and could be replaced by a list of the relevant genital part – e.g. Penis, prostate etc – and characteristics e.g. Deep voice, narrow hips, etc. This would remove the circularity.

Sometime a child is born with genitalia which can not be classified as female or male. A genetically child (ie. With xx chromosomes) may be born with external genitalia which appear to be those of a normal male. Or a genetically male child (xy chromosomes) may be born with female appearing external genitalia. In very rare cases, a child may be born with both female and male genitalia. Because these conditions are in some sense 'in between' the two sexes, they are collectively referred to as intersex. Various physical conditions can make people intersexed. The following are some of the most common conditions. Some people have 'xxy' chromosomes and consequently are born with male genitals but develop female secondary characteristics, such as breasts, at puberty. Other have 'xx' chromosomes but, due to exposure to excess androgens in the womb, their female internal genitalia are accompanied by ambiguous or male external genitalia. Other individuals with 'xy' chromosomes have androgen insensitivity syndromes (AIS). They have male internal genitals but their bodies do not respond to the androgens that their testes produce and so they develop more or less female external genitalia and body shapes.

John Wiener, a urologist, has suggested defining intersex simply as "a discordance between phenotypic sex and chromosomal sex."[1] While this definition would cover most true intersex patients, there are some rare conditions which are clearly intersex which are not captured by this definition. For example, some people are moraics: Different cells in their body have different chromosomes. A 46, xy/46, xx mosial is an individual in whom some cells have the male chromosomal complement (xy) and some cells have the female chromosomal complement (xx). If such an individual has both a penis and a vagina, then there is no mismatch between phenotypic sex and genotypic sex. Both the phenotype and the genotype are intersexual. Yet according to Wiener's definition, such an individual would not be intersex. A more comprehensive, yet still clinically useful definition of intersex would include those conditions in which (a) the phenotype is not classified as either male or female, or (b) chromosomal sex is inconsistent with phenotypic sex. This definition is of course more clinically focused than the definition employed by Fausto-Sterling using her definition of intersex as "any deviation from the Platonic ideal"[2] She lists all the following conditions as intersex (a) Late-onset congenital adrenal hyperplasia (LOCAH) (b) Klinefelter (xxy), (c) Other non-xx, non-xy, excluding Turner and Klinefelter, (d) Turner Syndrome (XO) (e) Vaginal agencies (f) Classic congenital adrenal hyperplasia (g) Complete androgen insensitivity (h) True hermaphroditer, (i) Idiopathic and (j) Partial androgen insensitivity. The chief problem with this list is that the five most common conditions listed are not intersex condition. If we examine these five conditions in more details, we will see that there is no meaningful clinical sense in which these conditions can be considered intersex. "Deviation from the Platonic ideal" is as we will see, not a clinically useful criterions for defining a medical condition such as intersex.

Among classic intersex conditions, the most common are congenital adrenal hyperplasia (CAH) and complete androgen insensitivity syndrome. According to Fausto-Sterling's figures, these two conditions occur with roughly the same frequency. There is no dispute that these conditions are indeed intersex conditions. We discuss them here because some understanding of these conditions is essential in order to perceive how these conditions differ from the other syndromes which Fausto-Sterling includes in the category of intersex.

These individuals are genetically male (XY), but owing to a defect in the androgen receptor, their cells do not respond to testosterone or other androgens.[3] As a result, these individuals do not form male genitalia. Genetically male (XY) babies with this condition typically are born with a vaginal opening and clitoris indistinguishable from those seen in normal female (XX) babies. In almost all cases, the diagnosis is not suspected until puberty, when these "girls" are brought to medical attention because they have never menstruated. Investigation at that point will invariably reveal that these "girls" are in fact genetically male, that they have undescended testicles, and that neither the uterus nor the ovaries are present. These individuals are genotypically male, but phenotypically female.

In the congenital Adrenal Hyperplasia syndrome, a defect in an enzyme involved in the synthesis of adrenal hormones leads to a blockage in one synthetic pathway, giving rise to excessive production of androgenic hormones in a different pathway.[4] These androgens will masculinize a female (XX) fetus in utero. At birth, the girl's genitalia may appear completely masculine, or, more commonly, the genitalia will be ambiguous—neither completely male nor completely female but somewhere in between.

Fausto-Sterling defines all sex chromosome complements other than XX or XY as intersex. Specifically, Fausto-Sterling includes Klinefelter syndrome, Turner syndrome, and all other non-XX, non-XY chromosomal variations in the intersex category.

Other chromosomal variants (non-XX and non-XY, excluding Turner's and Klinefelter's). This category includes a variety of sex chromosome complements, such as XXX, XYY, and other less frequent arrangements. Fausto-Sterling considers all such conditions to be intersex. Men with an extra Y chromosome (47,XYY) are not distinguishable from normal (46,XY) men, although the average intelligence of men with this aneuploidy is lower than normal. Their fertility usually is not impaired. They are most commonly discovered in the course of evaluation for mild mental retardation or behavior problems (Fryns, Kleczkowska, Kubien, & Van den Berghe, 1995). Likewise, women with an extra X chromosome ("triple X," 47,XXX) are fertile, although the mean intelligence of women with this aneuploidy is also probably below average.[5] None of these chromosomal variants are associated with ambiguous genitalia, or with any confusion regarding sexual identity. There is therefore no clinical sense in which these individuals are intersex.

Vaginal agenesis (also known as vaginal atresia), a condition in which the distal third of the vagina fails to develop and is replaced by about 2 cm of fibrous tissue[6] (Simpson, 1999). Vaginal agenesis is not an intersex condition. Girls born with this condition have an XX genotype and normal ovaries. In the majority of cases, vaginoplasty restores normal female vaginal anatomy (Robson & Oliver, 2000). Women who have undergone vaginoplasty can and do go on to have successful term pregnancies (Moura, Navarro, & Nogueira, 2000). Nosologically, vaginal agenesis is to genital anatomy as cleft palate is to maxillofacial anatomy. Surgical correction for vaginal agenesis is conceptually no different from surgical correction for cleft palate.

Intersex people are treated in different ways by different cultures. In some cultures such people were included in larger "third gender" or gender-blending social roles along with other individuals. In most societies, intersexed people have been expected to conform to either a female or a male gender role.[7]

The existence of intersex people was known to many ancient and pre-modern cultures. An example is one of the Sumerian creation myths from more than 4,000 years ago. The story has *Ninmah,* a mother goddess, fashioning mankind out of clay.[8] She boasts that she will determine the fate – good or bad – for all she fashions. *Enki,* the father god, retorts as follows.

Enki answered Ninmah: "I will counterbalance whatever fate – good or bad – you happen to decide." Ninmah took clay from the top of the abzu [ab = water, zu = far] in her hand and she fashioned from it first a man who could not bend his outstretched weak hands. Enki looked at the man who cannot bend his outstretched weak hands, and decreed his fate: he appointed him as a servant of the king.

> ... [Three men and one woman with atypical biology are formed and Enki gives each of them various forms of status to ensure respect for their uniqueness] ... .

Sixth, she fashioned one with neither penis nor vagina on its body. Enki looked at the one with neither penis nor vagina on its body and gave it the name Nibru [eunuch(?)], and decreed as its fate to stand before the king."

During the Victorian era, medical authors introduced the terms "true hermaphrodite" for an individual who has both ovarian and testicular tissue, verified under a microscope, "male pseudo-hermaphrodite" for a person with testicular tissue, but either female or ambiguous sexual anatomy, and "female pseudo-hermaphrodite" for a person with ovarian tissue, but either male or ambiguous sexual anatomy. In Europe, the term 'intersexual' was first to be used before the Second World War.[9] The first call to replace the term 'hermaphrodite' with 'intersex' came from British specialist Cawadias in the 1940s.[10] This suggestion was taken up by specialists in the UK during the 1960s, by both those who rejected Money's framework (then emerging from the USA),[11] and those who endorsed that approach.[12]

Since the rise of modern medical science in Western societies, some intersex people with ambiguous external genitalia have had their genitalia surgically modified to resemble either female or male genitals. It is ironic that, since the advancements in surgery have made it possible for intersex conditions to be concealed, many people are not aware of how frequently intersex conditions arise in human beings or that they occur at all.[13] Contemporary social activists, scientists and health practitioners, among others, have begun to revisit the issue, and awareness of the existence of physical sexual variation in human beings is returning.

The terms 'sex' and 'gender' means different thing to different feminist theorist and neither are easy or straight forward to characterized. The social construction framework explains that there is no essential universally distinct character that is masculine or feminine – behaviours are influenced by a range of factors including class, culture, ability, religion, age, body shape and sexual preference. Culture tends to divide the sexes, on the basis of gender, into distinct categories whose members are assumed to share particular abilities and personality traits. Gender is a structural feature of society more than an inherent concept, just like social class. Women, in the main, are still socialized towards undertaking the so called 'dependent' roles of wives and mother, while men are socialized towards regarding themselves as more independent and less nurturing than women and Intersex people whose social status is "female men"[14]. They do not have to behave or dress as men to have the social responsibilities and prerogative of husband and fathers:

> People who identify as transgender or transsexual are usually people who are born with typical male or female anatomies but feel as though they've been born into the "wrong body." For example, a person who identifies as transgender or transsexual may have typical female anatomy but feel like a male and seek to become male by taking hormones or electing to have sex reassignment surgeries.

People who have intersex conditions have anatomy that is not considered typically male or female. Most people with intersex conditions come to medical attention because doctors or parents notice something unusual about their bodies. In contrast, people who are transgendered have an internal experience of gender identity that is different from most people.

Many people confuse transgender and transsexual people with people with intersex conditions because they see two groups of people who would like to choose their own gender identity and sometimes those choices require hormonal treatments and/ or surgery. These are similarities. It's also true, albeit rare, that some people who have intersex conditions also decide to change genders at some point in their life, so some people with intersex conditions might also identify themselves as transgender or transsexual.

In spite of these similarities, these two groups should not be and cannot be thought of as one. The truth is that the vast majority of people with intersex conditions identify as male or female rather than transgender or transsexual. Thus, where all people who identify as transgender or transsexual experience problems with their gender identity, only a small portion of intersex people experience these problems.

It's also important to understand the differences between these two groups because in spite of some similarities they face many different struggles, including different forms of discrimination. The differences between transgender and transsexual and intersex have been understood by lawmakers in countries such as Australia where lawmakers have publicly acknowledged that people with intersex conditions have distinct needs from people who identify as transgender or transsexual.

Modern Western societies' transsexuals and transvestites are the nearest equivalent of these crossover genders, but they are not institutionalized as third genders.[15] Transsexuals are biological males and females who have sex-change operations to alter their genitalia. They do so in order to bring their physical anatomy in congruence with the way they want to live and with their own sense of gender identity. They do not become a third gender; they change genders. Transvestites are males who live as women and females who live as men but do not intend to have sex-change surgery. Their dress, appearance, and mannerisms fall within the range of what is expected from members of the opposite gender, so that they "pass." They also change genders, sometimes temporarily, some for most of their lives. Transvestite women have fought in wars as men soldiers as recently as the nineteenth century; some married women, and others went back to being women and married men once the war was over.[16]

Some were discovered when their wounds were treated; others not until they died. In order to work as a jazz musician, a man's occupation, Billy Tipton, a woman, lived most of her life as a man. She died recently at seventy-four, leaving a wife and three adopted sons for whom she was husband and father, and musicians with whom she had played and traveled, for whom she was "one of the boys".[17] There have been many other such occurrences of women passing as men to do more prestigious or lucrative men's work.[18]

Genders, therefore, are not attached to a biological substratum. Gender boundaries are breachable, and individual and socially organized shifts from one gender to another call attention to "cultural, social, or aesthetic dissonances"[19]. These odd or deviant or third genders show us what we ordinarily take for granted - that people have to learn to be women and men. Men who cross-dress for performances or for pleasure often learn from women's magazines how to "do" femininity convincingly.[20] Because transvestism is direct evidence of how gender is constructed, Marjorie Garber claims it has "extraordinary power... to disrupt, expose, and challenge, putting in question the very notion of the 'original' and of stable identity".[21]

Although the possible combinations of genitalia, body shapes, clothing, mannerisms, sexuality, and roles could produce infinite varieties in human beings, the social institution of gender depends on the production and maintenance of a limited number of gender statuses and of making the members of these statuses similar to each other. Individuals are born sexed but not gendered, and they have to be taught to be masculine or feminine.[8] As Simone de Beauvoir said: "One is not born, but rather becomes, a woman...; it is civilization as a whole that produces this creature... which is described as feminine"

Many cultures go beyond clothing, gestures, and demeanor in gendering children. They inscribe gender directly into bodies. In traditional Chinese society, mothers once bound their daughters' feet into three-inch stumps to enhance their sexual attractiveness. Jewish fathers circumcise their infant sons to show their covenant with God. Women in African societies remove the clitoris of prepubescent girls, scrape their labia, and make the lips grow together to preserve their chastity and ensure their marriageability. In Western societies, women augment their breast size with silicone and reconstruct their faces with cosmetic surgery to conform to cultural ideals of feminine beauty. Hanna Papanek[22] notes that these practices reinforce the sense of superiority or inferiority in the adults who carry them out as well as in the children on whom they are done: The genitals of Jewish fathers and sons are physical and psychological evidence of their common dominant religious and familial status; the genitals of African mothers and daughters are physical and psychological evidence of their joint subordination.

Sandra Bern[23] argues that because gender is a powerful "schema" that orders the cognitive world, one must wage a constant, active battle for a child not to fall into typical gendered attitudes and behavior. In 1972, Ms. Magazine published Lois Gould's fantasy of how to raise a child free of gender-typing. The experiment calls for hiding the child's anatomy from all eyes except the parents' and treating the child as neither a girl nor a boy. The child, called X, gets to do all the things boys and girls do. The experiment is so successful that all the children in X's class at school want to look and behave like X. At the end of the story, the creators of the experiment are asked what will happen when X grows up. The scientists' answer is that by then it will be quite clear what X is, implying that its hormones will kick in and it will be revealed as a female or male. That ambiguous, and somewhat contradictory, ending lets Gould off the hook; neither she nor we have any idea what someone brought up in a totally androgynous manner would be like sexually or socially as an adult. The hormonal input will not create gender or sexuality but will only establish secondary sex characteristics; breasts, beards, and menstruation alone do not produce social manhood or womanhood. Indeed, it is at puberty, when sex characteristics become evident, that most societies put pubescent children through their most important rites of passage, the rituals that officially mark them as fully gendered—that is, ready to marry and become adults.

Most parents create a gendered world for their newborn by naming, birth announcements, and dress. Children's relationships with same-gendered and different-gendered caretakers structure their self-identifications and personalities. Through cognitive development, children extract and apply to their own actions the appropriate behavior for those who belong in their own gender, as well as race, religion, ethnic group, and social class, rejecting what is not appropriate. If their social categories are highly valued, they value themselves highly; if their social categories are of low status, they lose self-esteem.[24] Many feminist parents who want to raise androgynous children soon lose their children to the pull of gendered norms.[25]

For human beings there is no essential femaleness or maleness, femininity or masculinity, womanhood or manhood, but once gender is ascribed, the social order constructs and holds individuals to strongly gendered norms and expectations. Individuals may vary on many of the components of gender and may shift genders temporarily or permanently, but they must fit into the limited number of gender statuses their society recognizes.

The pervasiveness of gender as a way of structuring social life demands that gender statuses be clearly differentiated. Varied talents, sexual preferences, identities, personalities, interests, and ways of interacting fragment the individual's bodily and social experiences. Nonetheless, these are organized in Western cultures into two and only two socially and legally recognized gender statuses, "man" and "woman." In the social construction of gender, it does not matter what men and women actually do; it does not even matter if they do exactly the same thing. The social institution of gender insists only that what they do is perceived as different.

If men and women are doing the same tasks, they are usually spatially segregated to maintain gender separation, and often the tasks are given different job titles as well, such as executive secretary and administrative assistant.[26] If the differences between women and men begin to blur, society's "sameness taboo" goes into action.[27] At a rock and roll dance at West Point in 1976, the year women were admitted to the prestigious military academy for the first time, the school's administrators "were reportedly perturbed by the sight of mirror-image couples dancing in short hair and dress gray trousers," and a rule was established that women cadets could dance at these events only if they wore skirts.[28] Women recruits in the U.S. Marine Corps are required to wear makeup - at a minimum, lipstick and eye shadow - and they have to take classes in makeup, hair care, poise, and etiquette. This feminization is part of a deliberate policy of making them clearly distinguishable from men Marines. Christine Williams quotes a twenty-five-year-old woman drill instructor as saying, "A lot of the recruits who come here don't wear makeup; they're tomboyish or athletic. A lot of them have the preconceived idea that going into the military means they can still be a tomboy. They don't realize that you are a Woman Marine" (1989, 76-77).[29]

If gender differences were genetic, physiological, or hormonal, gender bending and gender ambiguity would occur only in hermaphrodites, who are born with chromosomes and genitalia that are not clearly female or male. Since gender differences are socially constructed, all men and all women can enact the behavior of the other, because they know the other's social script: "'Man' and 'woman' are at once empty and overflowing categories. Empty because they have no ultimate, transcendental meaning. Overflowing because even when they appear to be fixed, they still contain within them alternative, denied, or suppressed definitions."[30] Nonetheless, though individuals may be able to shift gender statuses, the gender boundaries have to hold, or the whole gendered social order will come crashing down....

There is no core or bedrock human nature below these endlessly looping processes of the social production of sex and gender, self and other identity and psyche, each of which is a "complex cultural construction". For humans, the social is the natural. Therefore, "in its feminist senses, gender cannot mean simply the cultural appropriation of biological sexual difference. Sexual difference is itself a fundamental - an scientifically contested - construction. Both 'sex' and 'gender' are woven of multiple[31], asymmetrical strands of difference, charged with multifaceted dramatic narratives of domination and struggle"

For Scott, gender is a social system of meanings, produced around the biological sex by cultural and social factors. With this idea, it has been possible to give up essentialist and socio-biological theories of 'woman' and 'man' as natural, unhistorical entities and examine gender as a social construction.[32] In her critical analysis *Gender Trouble* (1990), Judith Butler attacks the idea of "a natural sex" as a politically neutral surface on which culture acts. Taken to its logical limit, the sex/gender distinction suggests a radical discontinuity between sexed bodies and culturally constructed genders, says Butler. She argues that the seemingly prediscursive construct called "sex" itself is a gendered category, which means that gender ought not to be conceived merely as the cultural inscription of meaning on a pregiven sex, but, instead, "gender must also designate the very apparatus of production whereby the sexes themselves are established."[33] Extending her critique to the question of the subject, Butler also challenges the feminist theories assuming a "doer" behind the deed. Since the "doer," according to Butler, is variably constructed in and through the deed, the substantive "I" only appears as such through a signifying practice, in a process of performative repetition of acts.[34]

Many people, including many feminists, have ordinarily taken sex ascriptions to be solely a matter of biology with no social or cultural dimension. It is commonplace to think that there are only two sexes and that biological sex classifications are utterly unproblematic. By contrast, some feminists have argued that sex classifications are not unproblematic and that they are not solely a matter of biology. In order to make sense of this, it is helpful to distinguish object- and idea-construction: social forces can be said to construct certain kinds of objects (e.g. sexed bodies or gendered individuals) and certain kinds of ideas (e.g. sex or gender concepts). First, take the object-construction of sexed bodies. Secondary sex characteristics, or the physiological and biological features commonly associated with males and females, are affected by social practices. In some societies, females' lower social status has meant that they have been fed less and so, the lack of nutrition has had the effect of making them smaller in size[35]. Uniformity in muscular shape, size and strength within sex categories is not caused entirely by biological factors, but depends heavily on exercise opportunities: if males and females were allowed the same exercise opportunities and equal encouragement to exercise, it is thought that bodily dimorphism would diminish.[36] A number of medical phenomena involving bones (like osteoporosis) have social causes directly related to expectations about gender, women's diet and their exercise opportunities.[37] These examples suggest that physiological features thought to be sex-specific traits not affected by social and cultural factors are, after all, to some extent products of social conditioning. Social conditioning, then, shapes our biology.

Second, take the idea-construction of sex concepts. Our concept of *sex* is said to be a product of social forces in the sense that what counts as sex is shaped by social meanings. Standardly, those with XX-chromosomes, ovaries that produce large egg cells, female genitalia, a relatively high proportion of 'female' hormones, and other secondary sex characteristics (relatively small body size, less body hair) count as biologically female. Those with XY-chromosomes, testes that produce small sperm cells, male genitalia, a relatively high proportion of 'male' hormones and other secondary sex traits (relatively large body size, significant amounts of body hair) count as male. This understanding is fairly recent. The prevalent scientific view from Ancient Greeks until the late 18th century, did not consider female and male sexes to be distinct categories with specific traits; instead, a 'one-sex model' held that males and females were members of the same sex category. Females' genitals were thought to be the same as males' but simply directed inside the body; ovaries and testes (for instance) were referred to by the same term and whether the term referred to the former or the latter was made clear by the context [38]. It was not until the late 1700s that scientists began to think of female and male anatomies as radically different moving away from the 'one-sex model' of a single sex spectrum to the (nowadays prevalent) 'two-sex model' of sexual dimorphism.

Fausto-Sterling has recently argued that this 'two-sex model' isn't straightforward either [39]. She estimates that 1.7% of population fail to neatly fall within the usual sex classifications possessing various combinations of different sex characteristics[40] (Fausto-Sterling 2000a, 20). These intersexed individuals make up (at least) three further sex classes: 'herms' who possess one testis and one ovary; 'merms' who possess testes, some aspects of female genitalia but no ovaries; and 'ferms' who have ovaries, some aspects of male genitalia but no testes [41](Fausto-Sterling 1993b, 21). Recognition of intersexes suggests that feminists (and society at large) are wrong to classify individuals only as female or male: there should be more than two sex categories.

To illustrate further the idea-construction of sex, consider the case of the athlete Maria Patino. Patino has female genitalia, has always considered herself to be female and was considered so by others. However, she was discovered to have XY chromosomes and was barred from competing in women's sports[42] (Fausto-Sterling 2000b, 1-3). Patino's genitalia were at odds with her chromosomes and the latter were taken to determine her sex. Patino successfully fought to be recognised as a female athlete arguing that her chromosomes alone were not sufficient to *not* make her female. Intersexes, like Patino, illustrate that our understandings of sex differ and suggest that there is no immediately obvious way to settle what sex amounts to purely biologically or scientifically. Deciding what sex is involves evaluative judgements that are influenced by social factors.

Insofar as our cultural conceptions affect our understandings of sex, feminists must be much more careful about sex classifications and rethink what sex amounts to[43] (Stone 2007, chapter 1). More specifically, intersexed people illustrate that sex traits associated with females and males need not always go together and that individuals can have some mixture of these traits. This suggest to Stone that *sex* is a cluster concept: it is sufficient to satisfy enough of the sex features that tend to cluster together in order to count as being of a particular sex. But, one need not satisfy *all* of those features or some arbitrarily chosen supposedly *necessary* sex feature, like chromosomes (Stone 2007, 44).[44] This makes sex a matter of degree and sex classifications should take place on a spectrum: one can be more or less female/male but there is no sharp distinction between the two. Further, intersexes (along with trans people) are located at the centre of the sex spectrum and in many cases their sex will be indeterminate (Stone 2007).[45]

In addition to arguing against identity politics and for gender performativity, Butler holds that distinguishing *biological* sex from *social* gender is unintelligible. For her, both are socially constructed:

If the immutable character of sex is contested, perhaps this construct called 'sex' is as culturally constructed as gender; indeed, perhaps it was always already gender, with the consequence that the distinction between sex and gender turns out to be no distinction at all. (Butler 1999, 10–11)[46]. (Butler is not alone in claiming that there are no tenable distinctions between nature/culture, biology/construction and sex/gender. See also: Antony 1998; Gatens 1996; Grosz 1994; Prokhovnik 1999.) Butler makes two different claims in the passage cited: that sex is a social construction, and that sex is gender. To unpack her view, consider the two claims in turn. First, the idea that sex is a social construct, for Butler, boils down to the view that our sexed bodies are also performative and, so, they have "no ontological status apart from the various acts which constitute their reality" (1999, 173).[47] *Prima facie*, this implausibly implies that female and male bodies do not have independent existence and that if gendering activities ceased, so would physical bodies. This is not Butler's claim; rather, her position is that bodies viewed as the material foundations on which gender is constructed, are themselves constructed *as if* they provide such material foundations (Butler 1993).[48] Cultural conceptions about gender figure in "the very apparatus of production whereby sexes themselves are established" (Butler 1999, 11).[49]

We can see that maintaining a distinction between the objective category of sexed identity and the varied and culturally contingent practices of gender does not presume an absolute distinction of the old-fashioned sort between culture and a reified nature. (Alcoff 2006, 175).[50]

That is, her view avoids the implausible claim that sex is exclusively to do with nature and gender with culture. Rather, the distinction on the basis of reproductive possibilities shapes and is shaped by the sorts of cultural and social phenomena (like varieties of social segregation) these possibilities gives rise to. For instance, technological interventions can alter sex differences illustrating that this is the case[51] (Alcoff 2006, 175). Women's specifically gendered social identities that are constituted by their context dependent positions, then, provide the starting point for feminist politics.

In an early article, though, Butler says she is in favour not of removing gender but of multiplying the number of genders. She recommends a Proliferation of Genders.[52] The idea is that, as well as the masculine and feminine ggenders, there might be others – transgendered and transsexual genders, perhaps and others besides. This view of Butler is convincing me. But other feminist have argued that multiple genders are impossible. Toril Moi argues that the word 'gender' refers to the systematic social organization of sexual difference – the imposition of only two general categories of being as normative for all people.[53] That is, Gender just is the norm that males should act masculine and females feminine. So if gender exists, then necessarily there can only be two ways to be gendered, Masculine and Feminine. Transgendered and Transsexual people are not, either actually or potentially, members of a new gender, rather, they cross over (in various ways) the feminine/masculine divide. Here again according to Butler that it undesirable to expect males to act masculine and females feminine, she is arguing that gender should be eradicated, not multiplied. Indeed, in the article in which Butler mentiones a 'proliferation of gender', what she actually seems to mean is a proliferation of styles of individual bodily behaviour. She thinks that it would be desirable for individuals to develop their own unique styles of bodily activity without being constrained to act either masculine or feminine. She is using the word 'gender' here to mean gener, individual styles of bodily action. The diversity of gender norms is limited by a heterosexual matrix of higher – level assumptions that (i) gender must express sex (ii) feminity and Masculinity must be sharply opposed and (ii) heterosexuality is normal because the gender ned one another as complements. My question here is if it is so than where do 'Interses' people go? What is their identity? What is their sex and what is their gender? Where do we fit them in the society? Are they not God gifted child like a boy and a girl, are they not naturally deserve their place in the society? There is 'He' and 'She' for man and woman, what pronoun is there for 'Intersex people'?

I would like to wind up this chapter by asking these questions to the society.

NOTES & REFERENCES

1. Wiener, J, S. (1999). Insights into the causes of sexual ambiguity. *Current Opnion in Uorology*, 9, 507-511)
2. Blackless *et al., op. cit.*, 200 p.161
3. Boehmer *et al.*, 2001
4. White P.C. (2001) Congenital adrenal hyperplasia. *Clinical Endocrinology ans Metabolism*, 15,17-41
5. Boehmer, A. L., Bruggenwirth, H., van Assendelft, C., Otten, B. J., Verleun-Mooijman, M. C., Niermeijer, M. F., et al. (2001). Genotype versus phenotype in families with androgen insensitivity syndrome. *Journal of Clinical Endocrinology & Metabolism*, 86, 4151-4160.
6. Simpson, J. L. (1999). Genetics of the female reproductive ducts. *American Journal of Medical Genetics*, 89, 224-239
7. Gagnon and Simon 1973.
8. The Electronic Text Corpus of Sumerian Literature". http://etcsl.orinst.ox.ac.uk/cgi-bin/etcsl.cgi?text=t.1.1.2#. Retrieved 2007-12-09
9. Hirschfeld, M. (1923) 'Die Intersexuelle Konstitution.' *Jahrbuch fuer sexuelle Zwischenstufen*, 23, 3–27
10. Cawadias, A. P. (1943) *Hermaphoditus the Human Intersex*, London, Heinemann Medical Books Ltd.
11. Armstrong, C. N. (1964) Intersexuality in Man. IN ARMSTRONG, C. N. & MARSHALL, A. J. (Eds.) *Intersexuality in Vertebrates Including Man*. London, New York, Academic Press Ltd.
12. Dewhurst, S. J. & Gordon, R. R. (1969) *The Intersexual Disorders*, London, Baillière Tindall & Cassell.
13. "Ambiguous Sex"—or Ambivalent Medicine? by Alice Domurat Dreger, *The Hastings Center Report*, May/June 1998, Volume 28, Issue 3 pp. 24–35
14. Amadiume, 111, 1987, *Male Daughters, Female Husband: Gender*

and Sex in an African Society, London, Zed Books.

15. Bolin, anne, 1987. "Transsexualism and theLimits of Traditional analysis." *American Behaviroal Scientist* 31, 41-65
16. Durova 1989; Freeman and Bond 1992; Wheelwright 1989.
17. Gender segregation of work in popular music still has not changed very much, according to Groce and Cooper 1989, despite considerable androgyny in some very popular figures. See Garber 1992 on the androgyny. She discusses Tipton on pp. 67-70.
18. In the nineteenth century, not only did these women get men's wages, but they also "hadmale privileges and could do all manner of things other women could not: open a bank account, write checks, own property, go anywhere unaccompanied, vote in elections" (Faderrnan 1991,44)
19. Garber, Marjorie. 1992. *Vested Interests: Cross-Dressing and Cultural Anxiety*. New York and London: Routledge
20. *Ibid.*
21. Garfinkel, Harold. 1967. *Studies in Ethnomethodology*. Englewood Cliffs, NJ.: Prentice-Hall
22. Papanek, Hanna. 1990. *To Each Less Than She Needs, From Each More Than She Can Do*
23. Bern, Sandra Lipsitz. 1981. "Gender Schema Theory: A Cognitive Account of Sex Typing." *Psychological Review 88*, 354-64
24. Chodorow, Nancy. 1974. "Family Structure and Feminine Personality." In Rosaldo and Lamphere, eds., *Women, Culture and Society*. Stanford, Calif.: Stanford University Press.
25. Gordon, Tuula. 1990. *Feminist Mothers*. New York: New York University Press.
26. Reskin, Barbara J. 1988. "Bringing the Men Back In: Sex Differentiation and the Devaluation of Women's Work." *Gender and Society* 7, 58-81
27. Rubin, Gayle. 1975. "The Traffic in Women: Notes on the Political Economy of Sex." In Rayna R[app] Reiter (ed.) *Toward an Anthropology of Women*, New York: Monthly Review Press.
28. Carol Barkalow's book has a photograph of eleven first-year West Pointers in a math class, who are dressed in regulation pants, shirts, and sweaters, with short haircuts. The caption challenges the reader to locate the only woman in the room

29. The taboo on males and females looking alike reflects the U.S. military's homophobia (Berubé 1989). If you can't tell those with a penis from those with a vagina, how are you going to determine whether their sexual interest is heterosexual or homosexual unless you watch them having sexual relations?

30. Scott, Joan Wallach. 1988, *Gender and the Politics of History*. New York: Columbia University Press

32. Joan W. Scott, Gender: A Useful Category of Historical Analysis', *American Historical Review* 91 (5), 1986, pp. 1067–1068; for the influence of Scott in Finland, see also Pirjo Markkola, 'Suomalaisen naishistorian vuosikymmenet', *Historiallinen Aikakauskirja* 1/2003, p. 61

33. Judith Butler, Gender Trouble (New York and London: Routledge, 1990), pp. 6–7, for the explicit critique of Joan W. Scott, see pp. 10, 152n17

34. *Ibid.*, pp. 25, 140–147

35. Jaggar, A., 1983, "Human biology inFeminist Theory: Sexual Equality Reconsidered", in C. Gould (ed), *Beyond Domination: New Persepectives on Women and Philosophy*, Lanham: Rowman & Littlefield Publishers, Inc

36. Fausto-Sterling, A., 1993a, Myths of Gender: Biological Theories about Women and Men, New York: Basic Books, 2nd edition

37. *Ibid.*

38. Laqueur, T., 1990, *Making Sex: Body and Gender from the Greeks to Freud*, Cambridge, Mass.: Harvard University Press.

39. ––, 1993b, "The Five Sexes: Why Male and Female are Not Enough", *The Sciences*, 33: 20–24

40. ––, 2000a, "The Five Sexes: Revisited", *The Sciences*, July/August: 18–23

41. ––, 1993b, "The Five Sexes: Why Male and Female are Not Enough", *The Sciences*, 33: 20–24

42. ––, 2003, "The Problem with Sex/Gender and Nature/Nurture", in S. J. Williams, L. Birke, and G. A. Bendelow (eds.), *Debating Biology: Sociological Reflections on Health, Medicine and Society*, London & New York: Routledge.

43. Stone, A., 2004, "Essentialism and Anti-Essentialism in Feminist

Philosophy", *Journal of Moral Philosophy*, 1: 135–153

44. Stone, A., 2004, "Essentialism and Anti-Essentialism in Feminist Philosophy", *Journal of Moral Philosophy*, 1: 135–153
45. Stone, A., 2004, "Essentialism and Anti-Essentialism in Feminist Philosophy", *Journal of Moral Philosophy*, 1: 135–153
46. —–, 1999, Gender Trouble, London: Routledge, 2nd edition
47. Campbell, A., 2002, *A Mind of One's Own: The Evolutionary Psychology of Women,* Oxford: OUP.
48. —–, 1993, *Bodies that Matter*, London: Routledge.
49. —–, 1993, *Bodies that Matter*, London: Routledge.
50. —–, 2006, *Visible Identities*, Oxford: OUP.
51. —–, 2006, *Visible Identities*, Oxford: OUP.
52. Butler Judith, "Variation on Sex and Gender: Beauvoir, Witti and Foucault." In *Feminism as critique*. Ed. Drucilla Cornell and Seyla Benhabib, Minneapolis, MN: University of Minnesto Press.
53. Moi, Toril. 1999, *What is a woman*? Oxford: Oxford University Press.

4

Intersex is not a Disease

Society in general tend to privilege individuals with male or female bodies so that the social position they subsequently occupy are better than the social position of those with intersex bodies. And this generates persistent sexist injustice and also generates their search for identity in the society. Intersex people faces an identity crisis, they are facing social segregation. They always have a common questions of why their gender is challenging, what is the need of treatment, is intersex a disease, why their natural body taken away and rearranged like sexual action figure. What is the need to feminize or masculinize the body?

Intersex is not a medical disorder. Intersex people are like anybody else; many will grow up and want relationships with members of the opposite sex, some will not. Some may want relationships with people who are the same sex; some may not feel happy staying the sex they were assigned as. There may be a higher chance of their not being happy with the sex they were assigned, and so it is important to be open and flexible about this as they grow up. If they do not feel comfortable in their assigned gender, there is nothing wrong in this, it is just how they are; the same goes for who they are attracted to when they get older.

Surgery should be avoided until children are of an age they can make their own decisions – unless for serious health issues. This is because any surgery reduces the options open to children when they grow up. If a child has ambiguous genitalia, they may wish to find love and companionship with someone who will appreciate them that way; or if they decide to change the sex that they were assigned, their options are better than if they have had surgery to confirm the original assignment.

Depending on the type of intersex condition, corrective surgery are performed not for protection of life or health but for aesthetic or social purposes. Unlike other aesthetic surgical procedures performed on infants, such as corrective surgery for a cleft lip (as opposed to a cleft palate), genital surgery may lead to negative consequences for sexual functioning in later life (such as loss of sensation in the genitals, for example, when a clitoris deemed too large/penile is reduced/removed), or feelings of freakishness and unacceptability, which would have been avoided without the surgery. In other cases, negative consequences may be avoided with surgery.

Opponents maintain that there is no compelling evidence that the presumed social benefits of such "normalizing" surgery outweigh the potential costs.[1] (Similar attitudes are present in some cases of botched infant circumcision, in which the solution might involve intensive medical and parental efforts to reassign the male baby to a female identity, which opponents claim lead to the degrading interpretation that females are essentially castrated males. This view overlooks the embryological origin of the penis/clitoris.)

Defenders of the practice argue that it is necessary for individuals to be clearly identified as male or female in order to function socially for them. However, many intersex individuals have resented the medical intervention, and some have been so discontented with their surgically assigned gender as to opt for sexual reassignment surgery later in life. The Declaration of Montreal first demanded prohibition of unnecessary post-birth surgery to reinforce gender assignment until a child is old enough to understand and give informed consent. This was detailed in the context of existing UN declarations and conventions under Principle 18 of The Yogyakarta Principles, which called on states to:

> Take all necessary legislative, administrative and other measures to ensure that no child's body is irreversibly

altered by medical procedures in an attempt to impose a gender identity without the full, free and informed consent of the child in accordance with the age and maturity of the child and guided by the principle that in all actions concerning children, the best interests of the child shall be a primary consideration.

What makes us "female" or "male," "girls" or "boys," "women" or "men"—our chromosomes, our genitalia, how we (and others) are brought up to think about ourselves, or all of the above? One of the first responses to the birth of a child of ambiguous sex by clinicians, and parents, is to seek to "disambiguate" the situation: to assign the newborn's identity as either female or male, surgically modify the child's genitalia to conform believably to that sex identity, and provide other medical treatment (such as hormones) to reinforce the gender decided upon. The assumptions that underly efforts to "normalize" intersexual individuals and the ethics of "treatment" for intersexuality merit closer examination than they generally receive.

A number of events have lately aroused substantial public interest in intersexuality (congenital "ambiguous sex") and "reconstructive" genital surgery. Perhaps the most sensational of these is the recent publication of unexpected longterm outcomes in the classic and well-known "John/Joan" case.[2] "John" was born a typical XY male with a twin brother, but a doctor accidentally ablated John's penis during a circumcision at age eight months. Upon consultation with a team of physicians and sexologists at the Johns Hopkins Hospital (circa 1963) it was decided that given the unfortunate loss of a normal penis John should be medically reconstructed and raised as a girl-"Joan." Surgeons therefore removed John/Joan's testes and subsequently subjected Joan to further surgical and hormonal treatments in an attempt to make her body look more like a girl's. The team of medical professionals involved also employed substantial psychological counseling to help Joan and the family feel comfortable with Joan's female gender. They believed that Joan and the family would need help adjusting to her new gender, but that full (or near-full) adjustment could be achieved.

For decades, the alleged success of this particular sex reassignment had been widely reported by Hopkins sexologist John Money and others as proof that physicians could essentially create any gender out of any child, so long as the cosmetic alteration was performed early. Money and others repeatedly asserted that "Johns" could be made into "Joans" and "Joans" into "Johns" so long as the genitals looked "right" and everyone agreed to agree on the child's assigned gender. The postulates of this approach are summarized succinctly by Milton Diamond and Keith Sigmundson: "(1) individuals are psychosexually neutral at birth and (2) healthy psychosexual development is dependent on the appearance of the genitals" . While not a case of congenital intersexuality, the John/Joan case was nevertheless used by many clinicians who treat intersexuality as proof that in intersex cases the same postulates should hold. The keys seemed to be surgical creation of a believable sexual anatomy and assurances all around that the child was "really" the assigned gender.

But reports of the success of John/Joan were premature-indeed, they were wrong. Diamond and Sigmundson recently interviewed the person in question, now an adult, and report that Joan had in fact chosen to resume life as John at age fourteen. John, now an adult, is married to a woman and, via adoption, is the father of her children. John and his mother report that in the Joan-years, John was never fully comfortable with a female gender identity. Indeed, Joan actively attempted to resist some of the treatment designed to ensure her female identity; for instance, when prescribed estrogens at age twelve, Joan secretly discarded the feminizing hormones. Depressed and unhappy at fourteen, Joan finally asked her father for the truth, and upon hearing it, "All of a sudden everything clicked. For the first time things made sense, and I understood who and what I was". At his request, John received a mastectomy at age fourteen, and for the next two years underwent several plastic surgery operations aimed at making his genitals look more masculine.[3]

Ethicists have ignored the question of intersex treatment because like most people they assume the phenomenon of intersexuality to be exceedingly rare. It is not. But how common is it? The answer depends, of course, on how one defines it. Broadly speaking, intersexuality constitutes a range of anatomical conditions in which an individual's anatomy mixes key masculine anatomy with key feminine anatomy. One quickly runs into a problem, however, when trying to define "key" or "essential" feminine and masculine anatomy. In fact, any close study of sexual anatomy results in a loss of faith that there is a simple, "natural" sex distinction that will not break down in the face of certain anatomical, behavioral, or philosophical challenges.[4]

Sometimes the phrase "ambiguous genitalia" is substituted for "intersexuality," but this does not solve the problem of frequency, because we still are left struggling with the question of what should count as "ambiguous." (How small must a baby's penis be before it counts as "ambiguous"?) For our purposes, it is simplest to put the question of frequency pragmatically: How often do physicians find themselves unsure which gender to assign at birth? One 1993 gynecology text estimates that "in approximately 1 in 500 births, the sex is doubtful because of the external genitalia."[5] I am persuaded by more recent, well-documented literature that estimates the number to be roughly 1 in 1,500 live births.[6]

The frequency estimate goes up dramatically, however, if we include all children born with what some physicians consider cosmetically "unacceptable" genitalia. Many technically nonintersexed girls are born with "big" clitorises, and many technically nonintersexed boys are born with hypospadic penises in which the urethral opening is found somewhere other than the very tip of the penis.

In a 1987 article on the ethics of killing one conjoined twin to save the other, George Annas suggested (but did not advocate) that one way to justify such a procedure would be to take "the monster approach." This approach would hold that conjoined twins are so grotesque, so pathetic, any medical procedure aimed at normalizing them would be morally justified.[7] Unfortunately, the present treatment of intersexuality in the U.S. seems to be deeply informed by the monster approach; ethical guidelines that would be applied in nearly any other medical situation are, in cases of intersexuality, ignored. Patients are lied to; risky procedures are performed without follow-up; consent is not fully informed; autonomy and health are risked because of unproven (and even disproven) fears that atypical anatomy will lead to psychological disaster. Why? Perhaps because sexual anatomy is not treated like the rest of human anatomy, or perhaps because we simply assume that any procedure which "normalizes" an "abnormal" child is merciful. Whatever the reason, the medical treatment of intersexuality and other metabolically benign, cosmetically unusual anatomies needs deep and immediate attention.

We can readily use the tools of narrative ethics to gain insight into practices surrounding intersexuality. There are now available many autobiographies of adult intersexuals.[8] Like that of John/Joan, whether or not they are characteristic of long-term outcomes these autobiographies raise serious questions about the dominant treatment protocols.

In the 1950s, a team of medical specialists at Johns Hopkins University developed what has come to be called the "optimum gender of rearing" system for treating children with intersex. The notion was that the main thing you had to do in cases of intersex was to get the gender assignment settled early, so kids would grow up to be good (believable and straight) girls and boys.

Under the theoretic leadership of psychologist John Money, the Hopkins team believed that gender was all about nurture—that you could make any child into a "real" girl or boy if you made their bodies look right early (before about 18 months of age), and made them and their parents believe the gender assignment. Though the Hopkins team wrote early on that children should be told the truth about their intersex histories in age-appropriate ways, in practice many medical care providers lied to patients or actively withheld medical history information from them.[9] Medical textbooks frequently gave doctors advice about how to lie to patients with intersex.[10] As the Hopkins model spread throughout the developed world, surgeons performed cosmetic genital surgeries on intersex children without their consent, believing this was necessary and efficacious. Endocrinologists, meanwhile, manipulated patients' hormones to try to get the bodies of patients to do what they thought was necessary not just for physical health, but for psycho-social health (i.e., getting the body to look sexually "normal").

To start with, lying to patients is not only unethical, it is bad medicine. Patients who were lied to figured that much out, and often stopped getting medical care they needed to stay healthy. (For example, some stopped taking hormone replacement therapy—critical after gonadectomy—and wound up with life-threatening osteoporosis at an early age.) They also suffered psychological harm from these practices, because they got the message that they were so freakish even their doctors could not speak the truth of their bodies to them. (A lot of doctors still have not told their present and former patients the name of their conditions. Some still withhold medical records from patients and from parents/guardians of minor children.)

The system was and is literally sexist: that is, it treats children thought to be girls differently than children thought to be boys. In this approach (still going on at Hopkins so far as we can tell), doctors' primary concern for children thought to be girls is preservation of fertility (not sexual sensation), and for children thought to be boys, size and function of the phallus.

The "standards" used for genital anatomy have been arbitrary and illogical. For example, under the "optimum gender of rearing" model, boys born with penises doctors considered small were made into girls—even though other doctors believed (and showed[11]) they could be raised as boys without castration, genital surgery, and hormone replacement. Girls with clitorises their doctors think are "too big" still find themselves in operating theatres with surgeons cutting away at their healthy genital tissue.[12]

Paradoxically, though all medical experts agree the identification of intersex anatomy at birth is primarily a psycho-social (not medical) concern, it is still treated almost exclusively with surgery. Parental distress is treated with the child being sent off to surgery. This is not an appropriate form of care for parents or children.[13]

There is no evidence that children who grow up with intersex genitals are worse off psychologically than those who are altered. In fact, there is evidence that children who grow up with intersex genitals do well psychologically. In other words, these surgeries happen before the age of assent or consent without real cause. "Ambiguous" genitalia are not diseased, nor do they cause disease; they just look funny to some people. There is substantial evidence that people who have been treated under the "optimum gender of rearing" model have suffered harm, psychological and physical. This does not mean doctors intended to harm their patients; far from it. But good intentions are inadequate reasons to maintain a practice that has shown to be unethical and unscientific.

Finally, parents consenting to intersex surgeries do not appear to be fully informed about the available evidence, about alternatives available to them, about the risks associated with surgeries, or about the theoretical problems underlying the "optimum gender of rearing" approach. For example, they are typically not told the evidence that gender identity may emerge to an important degree from prenatal hormonal actions on the brain—and thus, that you can't "make" a child a maintain a particular gender identity in the long term by doing surgery on him or her in infancy.[14]

The exact procedure of the surgery depends on what is the cause of a less common body phenotype in the first place. There is often concern as to whether surgery should be performed at all. A traditional approach to the management of intersexuality has been socially motivated surgery. However, some[15] (Alice Dreger) say that surgical treatment is socially motivated and, hence, ethically questionable; without evidence, doctors regularly assume that intersexed persons cannot have a clear identity. This is often taken further with parents of intersexed babies advised that without surgery their child will be stigmatized. Further, since almost all such surgeries are undertaken to fashion female genitalia for the child, it is more difficult for the child to present as male if they later select a male gender identity. 20-30% of surgical cases result in a loss of sexual sensation (Newman 1991, 1992).

As convention, surgery is performed at birth. Intersex advocates such as Anne Fausto-Sterling in her *Sexing the Body* argue surgery on intersexed babies should wait until the child can make an informed decision, and label operation without consent as genital-mutilation.

The common pathway of sexual differentiation, where a productive human female has an XX chromosome pair, and a productive male has an XY pair, is relevant to the development of intersexed conditions. During fertilization, the sperm adds either an X (female) or a Y (male) chromosome to the X in the ovum. This determines the genetic sex of the embryo.[16] During the first weeks of development, genetic male and female fetuses are "anatomically indistinguishable," with primitive gonads beginning to develop during approximately the sixth week of gestation. The gonads, in a "bipotential state," may develop into either testes (the male gonads) or ovaries (the female gonads), depending on the consequent events.[17] Through the seventh week, female and male fetuses appear identical. At around eight weeks of gestation, the gonads of an XY embryo differentiate into functional testes, secreting testosterone. Ovarian differentiation, for XX embryos, does not occur until approximately Week 12 of gestation. In normal female differentiation, the Müllerian duct system develops into the uterus, Fallopian tubes, and inner third of the vagina. In males, the Müllerian duct-inhibiting hormone MIH causes this duct system to regress. Next, androgens cause the development of the Wolffian duct system, which develops into the vas deferens, seminal vesicles, and ejaculatory ducts.[18] By birth, the typical fetus has been completely "sexed" male or female, the hormones and genital development remaining consistent with the genetic sex.

The final body appearance does not always correspond with what is dictated by the genes. In other words, there is sometimes an incongruity between genotypic (chromosomal) and phenotypic sex. Citing medical research regarding other factors that influence sexual differentiation, the Intersex Society of North America challenges the XY sex-determination system's assumption that chromosomal sex is the determining factor of a person's "true" biological sex.[19]

X/Y Name	*Description*
XXCongenital adrenal hyperplasia (CAH)	The most common cause of sexual ambiguity is congenital adrenal hyperplasia (CAH), an endocrine disorder in which the adrenal glands produce abnormally high levels of virilizing hormones. In people without a Y chromosome (i.e., XX), this can range from partial masculinisation that produces a large clitoris, to virilisation and male appearance. The latter applies in particular to Congenital adrenal hyperplasia due to 21-hydroxylase deficiency, which is the most common form of CAH. Individuals born with XX chromosomes affected by 17á-hydroxylase deficiency are born with female internal and external anatomy, but, at puberty, neither the adrenals nor the ovaries can produce sex-hormones, inhibiting breast development and the growth of pubic hair. See below for XY CAH 17á-hydroxylase deficiency.
XX Progestin-induced virilisation	In this case, the male hormones are caused by use of progestin, a drug that was used in the 1950s and 1960s to prevent miscarriage. These individuals normally have internal and external female anatomy, with functional ovaries and will therefore have menstruation. They develop, however, some male secondary characteristics and they frequently have unusually large clitorises. In very advanced cases, such children have initially been identified as males.[20]
	This condition occurs commonly in all species of cattle and affects most females born as a twin to a male. It is rare or unknown in other mammals, including

XX Freemartinism	humans. In cattle, the placentae of fraternal twins usually fuse at some time during the pregnancy, and the twins then share their blood supply. If the twins are of different sexes, male hormones produced in the body of the fetal bull find their way into the body of the fetal heifer (female), and masculinize her. Her sexual organs do not develop fully, and her ovaries may even contain testicular tissue. When adult, such a *freemartin* is very like a normal female in external appearance, but she is infertile, and behaves more like a castrated male (a steer). The male twin is not significantly affected, although (if he remains entire) his testes may be slightly reduced in size. The degree of masculinization of the freemartin depends on the stage of pregnancy at which the placental fusion occurs – in about ten percent of such births no fusion occurs and both calves develop normally as in other mammals.
XY Androgen insensitivity syndrome (AIS)	People with AIS have a Y chromosome, (typically XY), but are unable to metabolize androgens in varying degrees. Cases with typically female appearance and genitalia are said to have complete androgen insensitivity syndrome (CAIS). People with CAIS have a vagina and no uterus, cervix, or ovaries, and are infertile. The vagina may be shorter than usual, and, in some cases, is nearly absent. Instead of female internal reproductive organs, a person with CAIS has undescended or partially descended testes, of which the person may not even be aware. In mild and partial androgen insensitivity syndrome (MAIS and PAIS), the body is partially receptive to androgens, so there is virilization to varying degrees. PAIS can result in genital ambiguity, due to limited metabolization of the androgens produced by the testes. Ambiguous genitalia may present as a large clitoris, known as clitoromegaly, or a small penis, which is called micropenis or microphallus; hypospadias and cryptorchidism may also be present, with one or both testes undescended, and hypospadias appearing just below the glans on an otherwise

		typical male penis, or at the base of the shaft, or at the perineum and including a bifid (or cleft) scrotum.
XY	5-alpha-reductase deficiency (5-ARD)	The condition affects individuals with a Y chromosome, making their bodies unable to convert testosterone to dihydrotestosterone (DHT). DHT is necessary for the development of male genitalia in utero, and plays no role in female development, so its absence tends to result in ambiguous genitalia at birth; the effects can range from infertility with male genitalia to male underdevelopment with hypospadias to female genitalia with mild clitoromegaly. The frequency is unknown, and children are sometimes misdiagnosed as having AIS.[21] Individuals can have testes, as well as vagina and labia, and a small penis capable of ejaculation that looks like a clitoris at birth. Such individuals are usually raised as girls. The lack of DHT also limits the development of facial hair.
		In individuals with a Y chromosome (typically XY) who have Congenital adrenal hyperplasia due to 17 alpha-hydroxylase deficiency, CAH inhibits virilization, unlike cases without a Y chromosome
XX	Congenital adrenal hyperplasia (CAH)	The child has XY chromosomes typical of a male. The child has a male body and an internal uterus and fallopian tubes because his body did not produce Müllerian-inhibiting factor during fetal development.
XY	Persistent Mullerian duct syndrome (PMDS)	In addition to the most common XX and XY chromosomal sexes, there are quite a few other possible combinations such as Turner syndrome (XO), Triple X syndrome (XXX), Klinefelter's Syndrome (XXY/XXXY), XYY syndrome (XYY), de la Chapelle syndrome (XX male), Swyer syndrome (XY female), and there are many other individuals who do not follow the typical patterns (such as individuals with four or even more sex chromosomes).
	Less usual Other chromosomal sex	A mix can occur, where some of the cells of the body have the common XX or XY, while some have one of the less usual chromosomal contents above. Such a mixture is caused by either mosaicism or chimerism. In mosaicism, the mixture is caused by a mutation

	in one of the cells of the embryo after fertilization, whereas chimerism is a fusion of two embryos.
Mosaicism and Other chimerism	In alternative fashion, it is simply a mixture between XX and XY, and does not have to involve any less-common genotypes in individual cells. This, too, can occur both as chimerism and as a result of one sex chromosome having mutated into the other.[22] However, not all cases of mosaicism and chimerism involve intersex.

In the cases where nonfunctional testes are present, there is a risk that these develop cancer. Therefore, doctors either remove them by orchidectomy or monitor them carefully. This is the case for instance in androgen insensitivity syndrome.

Clearly, in our often unforgiving culture intersexuality can also threaten the patient's psyche; that recognition is behind the whole treatment approach. Nevertheless, there are two major problems here. First, clinicians treating intersex individuals may be far more concerned with strict definitions of genital normality than intersexuals, their parents, and their acquaintances (including lovers). This is evidenced time and again, for example, in theJohn/Joan case:

John recalls thinking, from preschool through elementary school, that physicians were more concerned with the appearance of Joan's genitals than was Joan. Her genitals were inspected at each visit to The Johns Hopkins Hospital. She thought they were making a big issue out of nothing, and they gave her no reason to think otherwise. John recalls thinking: "Leave me be and then I'll be fine.... It's bizarre. My genitals are not bothering me; I don't know why it is bothering you guys so much."[23]

Second, and more basically, it is not self-evident that a psychosocial problem should be handled medically or surgically. We do not attempt to solve the problems many dark-skinned children will face in our nation by lightening their skins. Similarly, Cheryl Chase has posed this interesting question: when a baby is born with a severely disfigured but largely functional arm, ought we quickly remove the arm and replace it with a possibly functional prosthetic, so that the parents and child experience less psychological trauma[24]? While it is true that genitals are more psychically charged than arms, genitals are also more easily and more often kept private, whatever their state. Quoting the ideas of Suzanne Kessler, the pediatric urologist Schober argues in a forthcoming work that "Surgery makes parents and doctors more comfortable, but counseling makes people comfortable too, and [it] is not irreversible." She continues: "Simply understanding and performing good surgeries is not sufficient. We must also know when to appropriately perform or withhold surgery. Our ethical duty as surgeons is to do no harmand to serve the best interests of our patient. Sometimes, this means admitting that a 'perfect' solution may not be attainable."[25]

Ironically, rather than alleviating feelings of freakishness, in practice the way intersexuality is typically handled may actually produce or contribute to many intersexuals' feelings of freakishness. Many intersexuals look at these two facts: (1) they are subject, out of "compassion," to "normalizing" surgeries on an emergency basis without their personal consent, and (2) they are often not told the whole truth about their anatomical conditions and anatomical histories. Understandably, they conclude that their doctors see them as profound freaks and that they must really be freaks. H. Martin Malin, a professor in clinical sexology and a therapist at the Child and Family Institute in Sacramento, California, has found this to be a persistent theme running through intersexuals' medical experience: They or their parents had little, if any, counseling. They thought they were the only ones who felt as they did. Many had asked to meet other patients whose medical histories were similar to their own, but they were stonewalled. They recognized themselves in published case histories, but when they sought medical records, were told they could not be located.... The patients I was encountering were not those whose surgeries resulted from life-threatening or seriously debilitating medical conditions. Rather, they had such diagnoses as "micropenis" or "clitoral hypertrophy." These were patients who were told-when they were told anything-that they had vaginoplasties or clitorectomies because of the serious psychological consequences they would have suffered if surgery had not been done. But the surgeries had been performed-and they were reporting longstanding psychological distress. They were certain that they would rather have had the "abnormal" genitals they [had] had than the "mutilated" genitals they were given. They were hostile and often vengeful towards the professionals who had been responsible for their care and sometimes, by transference, towards me. They were furious that they had been lied to.[26] Given the lack of long-term follow-up studies it is unclear whether a majority of intersexuals wind up feeling this way, but even if only a small number do we must ask whether the practice of deception and "stonewalling" is essentially unethical.

Why would a physician ever withhold medical and personal historical information from an intersexed patient? Because she or he believes that the truth is too horrible or too complicated for the patient to handle. In a 1988 commentary in the Hastings Center Report, Brendan Minogue and Robert Tarszewski argued, for example, that a physician could justifiably withhold information from a sixteen-year-old AIS patient and/or her parents if he believed that the patient and/or family was likely to be incapable of handling the fact that she has testes and an XY chromosomal complement.[27] Indeed, this reasoning appears typical among clinicians treating intersexuality; many continue to believe that talking truthfully with intersexuals and their families will undo all the "positive" effects of the technological efforts aimed at covering up doubts. Thus despite intersexuals' and ethicists' published, repeated objections to deception, in 1995 a medical student was given a cash prize in medical ethics by the Canadian Medical Association for an article specifically advocating deceiving AIS patients (including adults) about the biological facts of their conditions. The prize-winner argued that "physicians who withhold information from AIS patients are not actually lying; they are only deceiving" because they selectively withhold facts about patients' bodies.[28]

But what this reasoning fails to appreciate is that hiding the facts of the condition will not necessarily prevent a patient and family from thinking about it. Indeed, the failure on the part of the doctor and family to talk honestly about the condition is likely only to add to feelings of shame and confusion. One woman with AIS in Britain writes, "Mine was a dark secret kept from all outside the medical profession (family included), but this [should] not [be] an option because it both increases the feelings of freakishness and reinforces the isolation."[29] Similarly, Martha Coventry, a woman who had her "enlarged" clitoris removed by surgeons when she was six, insists that "to be lied to as a child about your own body, to have your life as a sexual being so ignored that you are not even given the decency of an answer to your questions, is to have your heart and soul relentlessly undermined."[30]

Lying to a patient about his or her biological condition can also lead to a patient unintentionally taking unnecessary risks. As a young woman, Sherri Groveman, who has AIS, was told by her doctor that she had "twisted ovaries" and that they had to be removed; in fact, her testes were removed. At the age of twenty, "alone and scared in the stacks of a [medical] library," she discovered the truth of her condition. Then "the pieces finally fit together. But what fell apart was my relationship with both my family and physicians. It was not learning about chromosomes or testes that caused enduring trauma, it was discovering that I had been told lies. I avoided all medical care for the next 18 years. I have severe osteoporosis as a result of a lack of medical attention. This is what lies produce."[31]

Similarly, as B. Diane Kemp- "a social worker with more than 35 years' experience and a woman who has borne androgen insensitivity syndrome for 63 years"notes, "secrecy as a method of handling troubling information is primitive, degrading, and often ineffective. Even when a secret is kept, its existence carries an aura of unease that most people can sense ... Secrets crippled my life."[32]

Clearly, the notion that deception or selective truthtelling will protect the child, the family, or even the adult intersexual is extraordinarily paternalistic and naive, and, while perhaps well-intentioned, it goes against the dominant trend in medical ethics as those ethics guidelines are applied to other, similar situations. In what other realms are patients regularly not told the medical names for their conditions, even when they ask? As for the idea that physicians should not tell patients what they probably "can't handle," would a physician be justified in using this reasoning to avoid telling a patient she has cancer or AIDS?

In their commentary in the Hastings Center Report Sherman Elias and George Annas pointed out that a physician who starts playing with the facts of a patient's condition may well find himself forced to lie or admit prior deception. "Practically," Elias and Annas wrote, "it is unrealistic to believe that [the AIS patient] will not ultimately learn the details of her having testicular syndrome. From the onset it will be difficult to maintain the charade."[33] They also note that without being told the name and details of her condition any consent the AIS patient gives will not truly be "informed." As an attorney Groveman too argues "that informed consent laws mandate that the patient know the truth before physicians remove her testes or reconstruct her vagina.[34]

It is not at all clear if all or even most of the intersex surgeries done today involve what would legally and ethically constitute informed consent. It appears that few intersexuals or their parents are educated, before they give consent, about the anatomically strict psychosocial model employed. The model probably ought to be described to parents as essentially unproven insofar as the theory remains unconfirmed by broad-based, longterm follow-up studies, and is directly challenged by cases like the John/Joan case as well as by evermounting "anecdotal" reports from former patients who, disenfranchised and labeled "lost to follow-up" by clinicians, have turned to the popular press and to public protest in order to be heard. Of course, as long as intersex patients are not consistently told the truth of their conditions, there is some question about whether satisfaction can be assessed with integrity in long-term studies.

At a finer level, many of the latest particular cosmetic

surgeries being used on intersexed babies and children today remain basically unproven as well, and need to be described as such in consent agreements. For example, a team of surgeons from the Children's Medical Center and George Washington University Medical School has reported that in their preferred form of clitoral "recession" (done to make "big" clitorises look "right"), "the cosmetic effect is excellent" but "late studies with assessment of sexual gratification, orgasm, and general psychological adjustment are unavailable ... and remain in question."[35] In fact the procedure may result in problems like stenosis, increased risk of infections, loss of feeling, and psychological trauma. (These risks characterize all genital surgeries.)

This lack of long-term follow-up is the case not only for clitoral surgeries; David Thomas, a pediatric urologist who practices at St. James's University Hospital and Infirmary in Leeds, England, recently noted the same problem with regard to early vaginal reconstructions: "So many of these patients are lost to follow-up. If we do this surgery in infancy and childhood, we have an obligation to follow these children up, to assess what we're doing."[36] There is a serious ethical problem here: risky surgeries are being performed as standard care and are not being adequately followed-up.[37] The growing community of open adult intersexuals understandably question whether anyone should have either her ability to enjoy sex or her physical health risked without personal consent just because she has a clitoris, penis, or vagina that falls outside the standard deviation. Even if we did have statistics that showed that particular procedures "worked" a majority of the time we would have to face the fact that part of the time they would not work, and we need to ask whether that risk ought to be assumed on behalf of another person.

Beginning in the late nineteenth century, medicine became the primary means for dealing with intersex. Before then, the vast majority of people with intersex conditions went unnoticed by legal, religious, or medical establishments and only a few cases per year came to the attention of authorities. Presumably other people with so-called "abnormal" sex anatomies lived average lives, either because their anatomical variance was undetectable or was not considered especially important. When a newborn had a high degree of genital ambiguity, midwives, grandmothers, and other local elders appear to have assigned the sex. (In terms of sexual orientation, all people were expected to then have sexual relations solely with those who had been identified as the "opposite" sex; in many places, violation of this rule was punishable by violent, sometimes fatal means.)

However, by the late 1800s, through gynecological sciences and numerous wartime military medical examinations, doctors gained a much better sense that "abnormal" sex anatomies were actually quite common. Indeed, late-nineteenth century medical men began reporting dozens of cases a year of "hermaphroditism" and "pseudo-hermaphroditism." Because most medical experts were politically conservative and wanted to keep sex borders clearly defined to combat open homosexuality and the rise of feminism, intersex caused them notable stress. (The conflation of sex, sexual orientation, and gender expression becomes clear in the 1890s use of the term "psychic hermaphroditism" to refer to gay men, and in the common "scientific" claim that university education physically "masculinized" women.) Therefore, biomedical specialists devised a system that would label everyone "truly male" or "truly female," regardless of the extent and natural reality of sexual blending.

Medical doctors created an arbitrary standard based on gonadal tissue, which persists in most medical texts today. A person with non-standard sex anatomy and ovaries is seen as a "female pseudo-hermaphrodite"; a person with non-standard sex anatomy and testes, is seen as a "male pseudo-hermaphrodite"; and if a person has ovarian and testicular tissue, they are seen as a "true hermaphrodite." Given the technological limitations of the time, Victorian doctors liked this system because they couldn't easily diagnose "true hermaphroditism" in living people; as a consequence, for the most part the only "true hermaphrodites" were dead and dissected people and the only medical information about intersex came from posthumous examinations.

All other people thought to be intersex, including pseudo-hermaphroditic, were labeled "truly male" or "truly female" and told to act socially and sexually normative in their assigned gender. However, with improved medical techniques and increased access to healthcare, many more people were being diagnosed with a biological "true sex" that made no sense socially. (In the 1910s as today, women with androgen insensitivity couldn't practically be labeled men just because they had testes.) And, in a bi-polar gender paradigm, there was no simple social category for those diagnosed with "true hermaphroditism." So, by the 1920s, experts treating intersex developed a notion of gender (social role) separated from biological sex. And they began to more actively offer surgical "corrections" to bring the biological sex into line with the assigned gender. So the theoretical approaches and surgical techniques evolved bit by bit, though motivation remained the same: keeping sex categories distinct and numbering only two.

It should be noted that, in the last half of the nineteenth century, a small percentage of patients with intersex had started to ask for, and some surgeons had started to offer surgical reconstruction of large clitorises, small vaginas, and hypospadic penises. With the exception of the rare clitorectomy performed on a child because she had a large clitoris, most of the genital surgeries performed for cosmetic reasons in the nineteenth century were performed on adults at their request. Both patients and surgeons generally avoided elective surgery for reasons of safety. There is also reason to believe that most people with intersex were socially healthy without surgery; they did not disproportionately live as hermits or attempt suicide. Psychologist John Money studied adults with intersex and found—before the era of standard cosmetic surgical intervention for intersex—that they enjoyed a lower rate of psychopathology than the general population.

Nevertheless, like many other realms of biology, sexuality, and psychology, intersex increasingly became the purview of medicine. For a small number of people with intersex—namely those at risk for gonadal cancers and salt-wasting—the medicalization of intersex probably improved their health, sometimes even saving their lives. Nevertheless, most of the treatment of intersex was motivated not by metabolic health concerns, but by psychosocial concerns; as in the 1890s, by the 1950s, intersex was viewed primarily as a psychosocial problem that mixed sex categories in socially uncomfortable ways.

In the 1950s, Johns Hopkins University created a team and became the first medical center to offer an organized multidisciplinary approach to intersex, one that sought to essentially eliminate intersex in early childhood. The approach developed there came to be known as the "optimum gender of rearing" model. The basic idea was that each child's potential for a "normal" gender identity should be maximized by making each child's body, upbringing, and mind align as much as possible. Because of the belief that it was harder to surgically engineer a boy than a girl, most children with intersex were made as feminine as possible, utilizing surgery, endocrinology, and psychology. A "successful" patient was one judged to be stable and "normal" (i.e., heterosexual) in the assigned gender. (In an era of vice squads raiding gay bars, it is not surprising that homosexuality appeared to most of these professionals an untenable identity.)

Though the early texts from this team advocated truth-telling and consistent psychological support, in practice many patients were deceived and given minimal psychological support. As in most of medicine, doctors made the decisions for patients. There was little investment in the ideas of informed consent or of studying outcomes in a systematic way. (It wasn't until the 1960s that medical professionals began aggressively looking for cases of intersex.)

Psychologist John Money provided theoretical support for the Hopkins model, arguing that gender identity was largely mutable early in life, that nurture was more important than nature. His chief support for this claim came from a famous case known as "John/Joan." The person at the center, David Reimer, was born an identical twin (not intersex) boy in 1965.

While performing a circumcision, a doctor accidentally burned off eight-month-old David's penis. David's parents consulted with the team at Hopkins, and Money recommended they change the sex and gender of their child and raise David as a girl. For decades Money erroneously touted a successful outcome because the child reportedly had become a normal, female-identified, heterosexual girl. The truth was that David had never felt fully female. Indeed, when his parents told him the truth about what happened to him, he immediately re-assumed the gender role of a man.

It is unknown why Money—who in 1953 had found a relatively low rate of psychopathology among adults with intersex—thought people with intersex needed to have their sexes and genders surgically and socially engineered to be psychologically healthy. It is better understood why people did not question Money's controversial theory of nurture-over-nature approach. Surgeons and psychologists liked the theory because it signified that they were providing necessary, good care to "abnormal" children. Feminists liked the theory because they preferred the idea that gender - and therefore gender norms - were socially constructed and malleable. Parents probably liked it because they could be reassured that their queer-bodied children would grow up to be straight-acting adults.

But some people didn't like this system: people who—like David Reimer—felt mistreated at best, and medically assaulted at worst, by their medical treatment. Nevertheless, most stayed silent, believing they were alone in their experiences.

That changed in 1993, when feminist biologist Anne Fausto-Sterling published articles in *The Sciences* and *The New York Times* exposing the basic fact that intersex exists. In response, Cheryl Chase wrote a letter to The Sciences announcing the founding of the Intersex Society of North America (ISNA). She founded the group because of her own attempts to recover her history of sex-reassignment in infancy and medically-induced shame, and because of the disinterest of most of her former care providers in what had happened to her. Soon Chase had brought together dozens of people with intersex.

Though ISNA began as a support group, it quickly turned into an advocacy group because its members realized that they had suffered from similar problems. Like many of the early ISNA members, Chase drew on her political consciousness as a lesbian woman to recognize the degree to which intersex had been unnecessarily socially and medically pathologized. With the successes of the women's health movement and the queer rights movements as a backdrop, people with intersex began agitating for openness and reform.

Early on, very few medical professionals recognized ISNA's critiques as legitimate. Many responded that the standard of care was necessary, successful, and justified, even going so far as to actively defend lying to patients about their medical histories. Those at the top simply tried to ignore ISNA. As the leader of the newly formed intersex rights movement, Chase moved rapidly, sometimes able to engage in dialog, and having group protests when doctors would not listen. With her professional background in computer science, she was particularly adept at using the tools of the Internet to spread ISNA's message. ISNA also supported the inquiries of researchers like Suzanne Kessler, Anne Fausto-Sterling, and Alice Dreger, and the organization engaged in media outreach as much as possible.

By about 2001, it had become clear to all that the intersex rights movement was not going away. The claims of activists were illustrated in story after story of problematic intersex treatment, as well as in research that strongly suggested gender identity is not simply a matter of nurture. The fact that medical professionals were unable to produce an intersex patient satisfied with his/her childhood treatment negated the claims that the advocacy groups solely represented the experiences of a disgruntled minority.

Finally, many medical professionals began to respond to calls for outcome data, research, full disclosure of information, and revision of homophobic and sexist protocols. The intersex rights movement undoubtedly was helped in its success by surrounding trends in favor of LBGT (lesbian, bi, gay, transgender) rights, patients' rights, and children's rights.

Since 1993, due to increased public education, tens of millions of people have learned about intersex. Thanks to the internet, thousands of people with intersex have mets others like them, in spite of having been told by their doctors they would never be able to do that—their conditions were supposedly so rare.

ISNA members have gone from picket lines to having a seat at the table in medical conferences. We give grand rounds presentations, help with medical school curricular development, and receive emails from physicians asking for our advice on how to handle intersex cases. Our website is recognized as the definitive source for all things intersex, and for being a life-saving porthold for thousands of people desperate for answers and directions to "their tribe". We have convinced hospitals around the world to examine their practices, to find out what has happened to former patients, and to be accountable for the sometimes-poor effects of good intentions.

Over a decade into the work of ISNA, medical professionals are less inclined to lie to patients and parents in intersex cases, are less likely to make openly homophobic or sexist remarks, and are more likely to admit uncertainty about the right course of action. A number of teams are engaged in active outcomes research, though opinions still differ about what outcomes should be sought; some think stable gender identity and heterosexuality are the objective; others suggest it should be lack of depression.) What type of care an individual or family will receive now varies dramatically; what happens to a child with intersex today appears to depend not only on where she or he is born, but who happens to be on call when she or he is born. But we're not done even today, the goal of many leading teams treating intersex is still to make intersex disappear. Pediatric endocrinologist Maria New, recommends Dexamethasone to women who may be carrying an XX child with CAH; these treatments do not alleviate CAH, it only makes the child's clitoris appear smaller (and, clinicians hope, makes the child less likely to grow up lesbian). Abortion is routinely offered to women who are likely pregnant with children with intersex conditions, including Klinefelter's Syndrome. Many surgeons maintain the paternalistic attitude that they should remove healthy testes from babies with AIS to "spare them the trauma later," thereby denying these girls the opportunity to have a natural puberty and to come to know themselves, in a sexual way, free from surgical scars. Many endocrinologists press unnecessary—sometimes devastating—"normalizing" hormone treatments on patients who are otherwise healthy. Finally, doctors continue constructing vaginas in infants and young children, despite arguments by many medical professionals that early vaginoplasties fail too often and are unnecessary to begin with.

By contrast, as in the women's rights movement, the civil rights movement, and the LGBT rights movements, the goal of intersex advocacy groups is to have people understand intersex conditions as human rights issues. ISNA maintains as its fundamental principle the principle also fundamental to the women's health movement and the LBGT rights movements: that one's genitals are primarily for one's own use, not for the comfort of others.

Intersex is a socially constructed category that reflects real biological variation. In other word, we can liken the sex spectrum to the colour spectrum. There's no question that in nature there are different wavelengths that translate into colours most of us see as red, blue, yellow, pink, orange. But the decision to distinguish, say, between orange and red-orange is made only when we need it – like when we are asking for a particular paint colour. Sometimes social necessity leads us to make colour distinction that otherwise seems incorrect or irrational, as for instance, when we call certain people 'black' or 'white' when they are not especially black or white as we would otherwise use the terms. In the same way, nature presents us with sex anatomy spectrums. Breasts, penises, clitorises, scrotums, labia, gonads – all these vary in size and shape and morphology sp called 'sex' chromosomes can vary quite a bit, too. But in human cultures, sex categories get simplified male, female and sometimes intersex, in order to simplify social interactions, express what we knew and feel, and maintain order. So, unfortunately nature doesn't decide where the category of 'Male' ends and the category of 'intersex' begins, or where the category of 'intersex' ends and the category of 'female' begins. Human (today, typically doctors) decide how small a penis has to be, or how unusual a combination of parts has to be, before it counts as intersex. Human decide whether a person with xxy chromosomes or xy chromosomes and androgen insensitivity will count as intersex.

The term "ambiguous genitalia" is always a matter of discussion because I think that no child thinks his or her genitalia are "ambiguous". They are just their natural or god gifted genitals. It's the grownups who are feeling ambiguous.

Intersex people are perfectly comfortable adopting either a male or female gender identity and are not seeking a genderless society or to label themselves as a member of a third gender class. Although it is true that the urge to perform surgeries on intersex children's sex anatomies is sometimes bornout of the belief that children must have sex anatomies that are clearly male or female in order to be comfortable in either a male or female gender and "I belief that this is clearly a harmful belief which is born out of antiquated notion about gender identity corresponding directly to genital anatomy. The shame that surround them are an unfortunate instantiation of problematic gender norms given by the society.

A lot of people think that doctors do 'normalizing' surgeries on infants children with intersex because, if they and didn't those children would grow up to be very damaged psychologically. Again here the psychological problem is directly associated with social problem. Because in our culture, sexual variation which blurs the line between male and female is stigmatized. The birth of an intersex child is emotionally traumatizing: Parents are traumatized because the birth of a child with sexual ambiguity violates a deeply held world view and because it elicits parental feelings of shame and quite. Parents are traumatized because "they are made to feel" I repeat the sentence "they are made to feel" (by the society) utterly unique, alone and unacceptable.

Gender is generally an identity issue. So intersex individuals should also have a natural right to have an identity in the society. Imagine a person with one blue eye and one brown eye. Such a person might seek out other like people and form an association. They might do this for any number of reasons including marginalization and discrimination. They might do it just to meet some one else with the same kinds of differences they have. They might even go so far as to make that a significant part of how they identify themselves. Whatever they do, if they make it a part of their identity or not, if they are marked out by society or not, if they form an association or not, they have one blue eye and one brown eye and only eye removal will change that. Even if they have their eyes removal the reasons for them having one brown eye and one blue eye remaining will be written in their bodied, in their genes. There natural identity remain the same. So where is the need to challenge (change) gender identity?

Intersex is not a medical condition, it is not a disorder or pathology or a condition of any sort. Intersex is just a difference in the same way colours, height, weight, and so on are differences. Only a very few ways of being intersex have links to differences that might cause illness. CAH (Congenital Adrenil Hyerplasia- are females capable of having a child with very few anatomical differences of sex) is common, strangely very few CAH individuals are intersex despite it being classified by medicine as a way of being intersex. We know of no XY CAH individuals who are intersex. Some intersex have very striking differences on anatomical presentation but they are usually very healthy and able people. There are lots of things intersex is not. If society accept intersex just as a physical difference than it will be easily dismiss those non-physical things that some might suppose are a part of intersex.

Intersex want 'Recognition' of intersex differences, that the ideal of the sex binary is flawed, that male and female are not absolute term and that insistence on sex binaries stigmatizes and marginalizes those who do not fit. Intersex people want equal rights at law. They want protection in human rights against discrimination on the basis of sex. They want laws to reflect the reality of their bodies so that they can have access to marriage, superannuation, insurance and all the things available to males and females. Intersex people want equal rights without having to pretend their bodies are really male or female.

Intersex people want an end to non-consensual infant surgery which is conducted to 'cure' the infant of intersex differences. The aim of this surgery is cosmetic. Very few infants have health problem because of their intersex anatomical differences. Intersex surgery seeks to make a child a penetrator or penetrate with aim of heterosexual intercourse as an adult. Intersex who go on to live in what appear to be same sex relationship are though to be a failure of assignment. The underlying paradigm of such surgery is homophobic. The alarm created when an intersex child is born cenres around whether the child will grow up to be a man or a woman and if they are neither then what kind of sexual role would they play? Now one might assume that there is a firm distinction between being transsexual and being transgendered. Transsexual, one might think, are those who change their sex or seek to change or are in the process of changing it through surgery and synthetic hormones. This is because they feel that their sex does not agree with their gender (stereotypically, they might feel like ' a man trapped in a female body). On the other hand one might think, a person is transgendered if they have an ambiguous gender identity and way of behaving. This ambiguity can take several forms. One's identity and behavior may include elements of both feminine and masculine genders. One's identity and behavior may not fit in with either genders. Or one might have a gender identity and way of behaving which conflict with what other people expect based on one's biological sex. For example, one might be a female who acts in a masculine way, jarring with most people's expectations that females should act feminine. In short, transgendered people are 'trangressivly gendered.[38] Transgendered need not involve changing from one gender to the other, as one might assume by analogy with transsexualism.

So transsex and transgender look clearly distinct, the former, it seems, involves changing sex; and the latter, it seems, involves having an ambiguous or transgressive gender. Intersex is not a part of transgender because intersex is about gender. Intersex is about anatomical differences in sex. There are some difference in the experience of transsexual and intersex individuals. There are some human rights protections and recognition at law for Transsexual people but not for Intersex. There are also certain rights like right to marry, superannuation, insurance and so on are available only for transsexual people but not for intersex. While some people with intersex conditions also identify as trans, intersex people as a group have a unique set of need and priorities beyond those shared with trans people. Too often, these unique needs are made invisible or secondary when 'intersex' becomes a subcategory of 'transgender'. For example, people who discuss about intersex in the context of transgender often stress the risk of assigning a 'wrong' gender as an argument against intersex genital mutilation, which overlooks the fact that intersex medical treatment is painful and traumatic whether or not one's gender idenuity happen to match her or his assigned gender. It is for this reason that intersex people prefer to have 'intersex' spelled out explicitly rather than have it included in the 'transgender' umbrella.

Intersex genitals are not a medical problem. They may signal and underlying metabolic concern, but they themselves are not diseased; they just look different. Metabolic concern should be treated medically, but intersexed genitals are not in need of medical treatment. The autonomy and right to self determination of the person with an intersex condition is violated by the surgery – centered model. In the concealment model, surgeries are done without truly obtaining consent; parents are often not told the failure rate, lack of evidentiary support for and alternatives to surgery. Social distress is a reason to change society, not the body of children, correcting the genitals tells us that they are wrong. Different is not wrong. Different is different. Identity shouldn't be centered around body parts. Therefore it is not enough to simply stop the surgery, there is a strong need to replace it with social and psychological support as well as open and honest communication and indeed is a strong need of the support of the government.

NOTES & REFERENCES

1. Intersex Society of North America (May 24,2006) what evidence is there that you can grow up psychologically healthy with intersex genitals (without normalizing surgeries)? Retreived 25 Nov. 2006

2. Milton Diamond and H. Keith Sigmundson, Sex Reassignment at Birth: Long-Term Review and Clinical Implications, *Archives of Pediatrics and Adolescent Medicine* 15 (1997): 298-304

3. For a more in-depth biography, see John Colapinto, The True Story of John/Joan, Rolling Stone, 11 December 1997, pp. 55ff

4. I discuss this at length in Dreger, *Hermaphrodites and the Medical Invention of Sex* (Cambridge, Mass.: Harvard University Press, 1998); see especially prologue and chap. 1

5. See Ethel Sloane, *Biology of Women*, 3d ed. (Albany: Delmar Publishers, 1993), p. 168. According to Denis Grady, a study of over 6,500 women athletes competing in seven different international sports competitions showed an incidence of intersexuality of one in 500 women, but unfortunately Grady does not provide a reference to the published data from that study (Denise Grady, "Sex Test," *Discover*, June 1992, pp. 78-82). That sampled population should not simply be taken as representative of the whole population, but this number is certainly higher than most people would expect.

6. Anne Fausto-Sterling, *Sexing the Body: How Biologists Construct Sexuality* (New York: Basic Books, forthcoming 1999), chap. 2; Fausto-Sterling, "How Dimorphic Are We?" American Journal of Human Genetics (forthcoming); and personal communication. The highest modern-day estimate for frequency of sexually ambiguous births comes from John Money, who has posited that as many as 4 percent of live births today are of "intersexed" individuals (cited in Anne Fausto-Sterling, "The Five Sexes," The Sciences 33 [1993]: 20-25). Money's categories tend to be exceptionally broad and poorly defined, and not representative of what most medical professionals today would consider to be "intersexuality."

7. George J. Annas, "Siamese Twins: Killing One to Save the Other" (At Law), *Hastings Center Report 17*, no. 2 (1987): 2729

8. See, for example, M. Morgan Holmes, "Medical Politics and Cultural Imperatives: Intersex Identities beyond Pathology and Erasure" (M.A. Thesis, York University, 1994); Chase, "Hermaphrodites with Attitude"; Geoffrey Cowley, "Gender Limbo," Newsweek, 19 May 1997, pp. 64-66; Natalie Angier, "New Debate Over Surgery on Genitals," New York Times, 13 May 1997; "Special Issue: Intersexuality," Chrysalis: The Journal of Transgressive Gender Identities 2 (1997). Intersexual autobiographies are also from peer support groups, including the Intersex Society of North America. For information about support groups see the special issue of Chrysalis, vol. 2, 1997

9. For examples of people who were lied to and deceived, check out Hermaphrodites Speak and Chrysalis.

10. For documentation, see Alice Domurat Dreger, Ambiguous Sex—or Ambivalent Medicine? Ethical Issues in the Treatment of Intersexuality. *Hastings Center Report*, 28, 3 (May/June 1998): 24-35.

11. For evidence boys with small penises do well without sex reassignment, see Justine M. Reilly and C. R. J. Woodhouse, "Small Penis and the Male Sexual Role," *Journal of Urology*, 142 (1989): 569-571, and see the autobiography of Hale Hawbecker in Intersex in the Age of Ethics.

12. See what UCSF's Laurence Baskin and Indiana's Richard Rink had to say at the American Academy of Pediatrics Urology Section's 2004 annual meeting.

13. See Edmund G. Howe, "Intersexuality: What Should Care Providers Do Now," *Journal of Clinical Ethics*, 9, 4 (Winter 1998): 337-344, reprinted in *Intersex in the Age of Ethics*.

14. On this point, see William G. Reiner and John P. Gearhart, "Discordant sexual identity in some genetic males with cloacal exstrophy assigned to female sex at birth," *New England Journal of Medicine*, 350, 4 (Jan. 22, 2004): 333-341, summarized and reviewed by Vernon Rosario; see also our FAQ Who was David Reimer?; and see *Pediatric Assignment of Sex: A Critical Reappraisal*.

15. Holmes M. (2002). Rethinking the Meaning and Management of Intersexuality. *Sexualities*, 159–180.

16. Kolodny, Robert C.; Masters, William H.; Johnson, Virginia E. (1979). *Textbook of Sexual Medicine* (1st ed.). Little, Brown and Company.

17. Kolodny, Robert C.; Masters, William H.; Johnson, Virginia E. (1979). *Textbook of Sexual Medicine* (1st ed.). Little, Brown and Company

18. Kolodny, Robert C.; Masters, William H.; Johnson, Virginia E. (1979). *Textbook of Sexual Medicine* (1st ed.). Little, Brown and Company.

19. Intersex Society of North America (May 24, 2006). Does having a Y chromosome make someone a man?. Retrieved 25 November 2006

20. "2000 Intersex Society of North America – What is Progestin Induced Virilisation?". Healthyplace.com. 2007-08-09.

21. "eMedicine article on 5-ARD". Emedicine.com. 2009-06-23. http://www.emedicine.com/ped/topic1980.htm. Retrieved 2009-08-21.

22. De Marchi M, Carbonara AO, Carozzi F, *et al.* (1976). "True hermaphroditism with XX/XY sex chromosome mosaicism: report of a case". *Clin. Genet.* 10 (5): 265–72. PMID 991437

23. Diamond and Sigmundson, "Sex Reassignment," pp. 300301

24. Cheryl Chase, personal communication.

25. Quoted in Justine M. Schober, "Long-Term Outcomes, for Intersex," in Pierre D. E. Mouriquand (ed.) *Pediatric Surgery and Urology: Long Term Outcomes*, (Philadelphia: William B. Saunders, forthcoming).

26. H. M. Malin, personal communication of 1 January 1997 to Justine M. Schober, quoted in Schober, "Long-Term Outcome."

27. Brendan P Minogue and Robert Taraszewski, "The Whole Truth and Nothing But the Truth?" (Case Study), *Hastings Center Report* 18, no. 5 (1988): 34-35.

28. Anita Natarajan, Medical Ethics and Truth Telling in the Case of Androgen Insensitivity Syndrome, *Canadian Medical Association Journal* 154 (1996): 568-70. (For responses to Natarajan's recomendations by AIS women and a partner of an AIS woman, see *Canadian Medical Association Journal* 154 [1996]: 1829-33.)

29. Anonymous, Be Open and Honest with Sufferers, *British Medical Journal* 308 (1994): 1041-42
30. Martha Coventry, Finding the Words, Chrysalis: *The Journal of Transgressive Gender Identities* 2 (1997): 27-30
31. Sherri A. Groveman, Letter to the Editor, *Canadian Medical Association Journal 154* (1996): 1829, 1832
32. B. Diane Kemp, Letter to the Editor, *Canadian Medical Association Journal* 154 (1996): 1829.
33. Sherman Elias and George J. Annas, "The Whole Truth and Nothing But the Truth?" (Case Study), *Hastings Center Report* 18, no. 5 (1988): 35-36, p. 35.
34. Groveman, "Letter to the Editor," p. 1829.
35. Newman, Randolph, and Anderson, *Surgical Management*, p. 651.
36. "Is Early Vaginal Reconstruction Wrong for Some Intersex Girls?" *Urology Times* (February 1997): 10-12.
37. Intersexuals are understandably tired of hearing that "long-term follow-up data is needed" while the surgeries continued to occur. On this, see especially the guest commentary by David Sandberg, "A Call for Clinical Research," Hermaphrodites with Attitude (Fall/Winter 1995-1996): 8-9, and the many responses of intersexuals in the same issue.
38. Bornstein, Kate,. 1994, *Gender Outlaw. On Men, Women, and the Rest of Us*. London and New York: Routledge.

5

Intersex in India

There is a common belief that the Hijras are born hermaphrodites. In India, hijras viewed as an institutionalized "third sex" that has always existed. They are particularly associated with the worship of 'Bahuchara Mata' and Lord Shiva. Bahuchara Mata, the mother of Goddess, cut her breasts off when attacked by an enemy. Shiva is believed to have castrated himself and then, throwing his 'Linga' into the world, spread his sexual power to the universe. His act results in the fertility cult of linga worship, which expresses the paradoxical theme of creative asceticism.[1] Whereas the ritual sacrifice of the Phallus associated with Shiva is at the deeper level of the hijras claim to power, it is at the more conscious and culturally elaborated level of devotion to the mother Goddess that is the centre of the hijras community and the focus for their sources of power. Their presence in society is justified by many Hindu myths. For one of the forms of the God Shiva is that of 'Ardhanarisvara', half man; half woman, who represents Shiva united with his 'Sakhi', or female creative power. Another mythological reference, often pointed to by hijras as the story of their origin, is contained in the epic *Mahabharata*, while in exile, the main character Arjun disguises himself as an eunuch and serves the ladies of the court. During this time, he participates in weddings and births, this legitimizing the roles hijras play in ritual contexts. Male transvestism is also a part of several esoteric Hindu ritual practice. For example, the Sakhibhava worship Radha, Krishna's beloved, with the aim of becoming her attendant. The devotee imitates feminize behaviour, including simulated menstruation; he may also engage in sexual acts with men as act of devotion;

and some devotees even castrate themselves in order to more closely approximate ,identification with Radha.[2]

Finally, hijras are mentioned in the *Kamasutra*, which contains an entire chapter on how to receive pleasure from a eunuch.[3] Hijras clearly have an accepted status within Hindu mythology and culture. In western culture hijras are known as homosexual. Hijras are not transsexual because they do view themselves as woman trapped in men's bodies. The emasculation operation does not transform them from men to women, but from men to hijras. They are neither man nor women because their lack of female reproductive organs and their inability to bear children, which for them is the criterion for womanhood. But it is also true that not all hijras undergo emasculation (total removal of penis, testes and scrotum in men) and the percentage of hijras that are eunichs is unknown. The operation referred to by hijras as a *nirvana* (rebirth) and carried out by a dai (traditional midwife) – involves removing the penis and scrotum with a knife without anesthesia. The cry and wail of the devotee is covered with loud trumpet. In the modern times, some hijras may undergo a vaginoplasty, allowing them to experience vaginal intercourse, but such cases are rare.

One may ask here, a very important question as whether we can consider Hijra as intersex person? Or whether hijra is also fall under the category of intersex people? My answer is 'yes', we can consider hijra as intersex because some of them are born intersex. According to Mumbai Health Organization the Humsafar Trust, only eight percent of hijras visiting their clinic are nirwaan (castrated). It means that the rest of the hijras in India, are born hermaphrodites. Therefore we can say that roughly 80% of hijras in India are hermaphrodites. However, in general hijras are born with typically male physiology, only a few having been born with male intersex variations.[4]

Hijras or eunuchs are considered as India's Third Gender. Today there are approximate one million eunuchs living in India, the only country where the hijra tradition persists. Having been prevalent since thousands of years, the community has fiercely clung on to its age-old tradition and rituals. There are different kinds of hijras in India. Hijras include people born with a male body, but with a non-male or female gender identity; transgender; transsexual or androgynous people; individual born with ambiguous genitalia (intersex or hermaphrodites); and individuals who have had castration / genital reassignment surgery performed on them. Hijras say that the genital severing happens with consent; people who do not like hijras say that the same sometimes happen forcibly. At the same time hijras have other names also; like in the Punjab and much of northern India they are known as Khusra or Khoti or Chhakka, while in Tamil Nadu they are called Aruvani. All of these names are now considered preferably to the English term, "Eunuch". They usually refer to themselves as female at the language level.

In this book I am basically concern with intersex people or born hijras not with those male who became hijra by castration–genital reassignment surgery. Hijras in India recently gained the right to officially note their gender as "E" on government forms and passports, and while running for public office. Hijras are an endemic part of South Asian culture, while the concept of homosexuality is only recently gained visibility.

I would like to share with you some of the experience of Hijra's while will give you some idea of the problems associated with hijras.[5]

Vidya

I am 39 and a graduate in hotel management. Somewhere deep in my heart I wanted to be female, so one morning aged 16 I went to be castrated. I now have another hijra staying with me and six or seven chelas, or followers. I am their guru. I am educated so have had many options, but 98% of hijras are illiterate and don't know what to do.

Kajol

I am 21 and became a hijra three years ago. We don't have proper sex change operations in India, so I had castration. We hijras have only two options – begging or sex work. I am a sex worker and I don't feel it's a bad thing to be one. I always liked cross-dressing. I work in an NGO doing very important rights work helping hijras and female sex.

Famila

Though hijras have existed so long, the law speaks about only two genders. We can't get ration cards, passports or voter IDs. Sex work is my only option.[6] Being a eunuch in this world spells discrimination. I grew up as one of them without education. Why? The reason was that I was refused admission in schools because of me being a eunuch. Like everyone I also had the desire to read and write. Without education I grew up and had no way to earn a living. I was unwanted and cursed. Most of the time I go to dark corners and wave to men and call them. Then take them to a roadside secret place and give them the sexual satisfaction they need. Only after they are satisfied I get paid. Old age is now tormenting me. What should I do other than getting involved in illegal activities or begging? Am I not human? Does human mean only men and women? Why are we deprived of humanity?

Sandhya

I am from Kolkata. My family consists of two brothers and three sisters. Even as a child, I loved dancing, wearing girls clothing, and using cosmetics. Whenever I acted in plays, it was a foregone conclusion that it would be me who would enact the role of the girl. I came to Delhi and merged into the hijra community after the death of my father. I, my giriya (husband), my mother and one of my sisters share one home. I have been living with my giriya for the past fifteen years and work as a pan toli. My giriya works in a production house and a part of the pooled earnings go to my giriya's ex–wife and child.

Prior to meeting my giriya, I was married twice. My wife, unable to conceive because of my biological condition ultimately divorced me. One of my strong characteristics is that I am highly opinionated. As a hijra I do not pay attention to the obscene remarks directed at me. I say, "Let them say whatever they feel like–it doesn't make any difference to me. What you see is what you get."

I began to visit the Sahara transgender project for treatment of the many minor illnesses that befell me. In due course, learning of Sahara's expertise in weaning people off narcotic and alcohol addiction, I confessed my dependence on liquor. I now have a health care worker assigned to me full time and part of my care package involves receiving, understanding and practicing safer behaviors related to sex and alcohol use. Though I suspect that I could be *HIV* positive due to the extent of my exposure to the virus, I have as yet not consented to test. Sahara is in no hurry preferring to wait until I am ready and have made an informed and definite choice.[7]

It is a general observation that large number of children with intersex disorder born in India do not receive medical attention during infancy. Department of Endocrinology and Metabolism, All India Institute of Medical Sciences, tried to assess the reason for this from the parents of children with intersex disorder and the affected individuals. The reason that were given by parents were –

- *Fear of Hijras.* It is believed that if the Hijras get to know the child has ambiguous genitalia they will take away the child.
- *Lack of awareness.* Large number of deliveries are conducted at home, sometimes even without a trained birth attendant. The parents often do not know where to go for help when they realize there is a problem.
- *Ashamed/afraid.* Parents are afraid/confused/ashamed to talk about the problem of their child and seek help.
- *Inadequate/inappropriate medical facilities.* There are only few hospitals in India which has trained manpower and facilities to investigate and treat children with genital ambiguity. So they need to travel long distance and incur lot of expenses.
- *Improper neonatal/child care.* We had two subjects who had traumatic castration as they were left unattended during early childhood.

Something, however, is beginning to alter in the traditional Indian mindset as right now there seems to be both subtle and appreciable changes taking place in terms of how this group are being treated and recognised by mainstream society. Over the last few months India has seen its first transgender fashion model, a transgender television presenter and in the recent Bollywood epic *Jodhaa Akbar* a hijra, instead of hamming up the usual comic role, was portrayed as a trusted lieutenant of the female lead.

Yet these developments come after years of crushing social stigmatisation, abuse and general derision from the wider community. Pooja, 27, realises there is still a long way to go: They make documentaries about us and say all these interesting things, but when we walk out on the street we still get the calling and the whistles.

The uphill struggle for the hijras first begins with finding acceptance within the family. My family didnt know I was castrated, tells Chandini, 28. My hijra friends teased me because I still went home in men's clothes, so I decided to go home as I am. When I got there some people in the street spotted me and told my mother, Here's your son! She saw me and fainted. My father came, he said, I don't have a son, go away! I lifted my saree and showed him. I said, "I'm not your son, I'm your daughter now."

Once the truth is out, hijras are usually forced to leave the family home. Yet the society they must take refuge in is equally as unwelcoming. Hijras have few rights and are not recognised by Indian law. This denies them the right to vote, the right to own property, the right to marry and the right to claim formal identity through any official documents such as a passport or driving license. Accessing healthcare, employment or education becomes almost impossible. In the face of such odds they are forced to earn money any way they can. In the day we go around the shops and beg," says Deepa. "They give us a rupee each and we go away. Sometimes we dance at weddings and festivals, we can get good money from this."

Since 2006, hijras in the state of Bihar have been employed by the government as tax collectors, singing loudly about the debt outside the defaulter's premises until they are shamed into paying up " one of the most effective tax recovery methods ever used in India. Yet for many hijras the method of making ends is prostitution. At night I go with the men," Pooja says. "I am looking good so I can get a room. Many who don't look so good must use the vehicles or somewhere else outside. Yes, it can be bad at times but I'm happy with this work."

As is the case for all gay, lesbian and bisexual people living in India, simply by being sexually active hijras are breaking the law. Section 377 of the Indian Penal Code (IPC) outlaws any 'carnal intercourse against the order of nature' " in other words, any sex that is not between a man and a woman with the aim of reproduction. Brought in by the British in 1860 to try and curb the 'heathen customs' of the local population, it carries with it a potential life sentence.

Whilst attitudes in the UK have matured considerably and such legislation has long since been removed from the British statute books, it still remains very much part of the Indian system. Although convictions are rare, it is in the name of such a law that the police are able to carry out their worst abuses against the hijra community. It seems that every hijra in India has her own story to tell of police brutality: "Once a policewoman attacked me," remembers Chandini. She said, "Why are you standing here?" and continued hitting me so I grabbed her hand and she ran away. She came back with two policemen and they took me to the station. There they beat me, stripped me and made me dance."

As well as the police aggression, gangs of local thugs known as 'goondas' frequently rob and sexually assault hijras on the street. These attacks are rarely prevented or reported by the locals. The local people I spoke with whilst reporting this story were all apprehensive, amused or downright hostile. 'They are a nuisance!' says Akram, a jeweler from Mysore. 'They come to your shop and when you don't give them money they lift up their sarees.' Later he adds, ' I've heard they even steal babies from hospitals.'

Until very recently these attitudes were mirrored and strengthened by the Indian media which itself seemed to suffer from a certain amount of gender vertigo. Hijras were routinely portrayed as wily tricksters who led unsuspecting men astray or half-man half-woman freak shows, almost devilish in their customs and practices. In 2003, an HIV/AIDS and human rights research centre in Lucknow was raided and the coordinator jailed under IPC 377 for "conspiracy to promote homosexual activities". An English language newspaper ran the headline: Gay Racket Busted- 2 NGOs Caught in the Act.

Most hijras live at the margins of society with very low status; the very word "hijra" is sometimes used in a derogatory manner. Few employment opportunities are available to hijras. Many get their income from performing at ceremonies, begging, or sex work—an occupation of eunuchs also recorded in premodern times. Violence against hijras, especially hijra sex workers, is often brutal, and occurs in public spaces, police stations, prisons, and their homes.[8] As with transgender people in most of the world, they face extreme discrimination in health, housing, education, employment, immigration, law, and any bureaucracy that is unable to place them into male or female gender categories.[9]

Beginning in 2006, hijras were engaged to accompany Patna city revenue officials to collect unpaid taxes, receiving a 4 percent commission.[10]

Hijras are often encountered on streets, trains, and other public places demanding money from people. If refused, the hijra may attempt to embarrass the man into giving money, using obscene gestures, profane language, and even sexual advances. In India for example, threatening to open their private parts in front of the man if he does not donate something. Hijras also perform religious ceremonies at weddings and at the birth of male babies, involving music, singing, and sexually suggestive dancing. These are intended to bring good luck and fertility. Although hijras are most often uninvited, the host usually pays the hijras a fee. Many fear the hijras' curse if they are not appeased, bringing bad luck or infertility, but for the fee they receive, they can bless goodwill and fortune on to the newly born. Hijras are said to be able to do this because, since they do not engage in sexual activities, they accumulate their sexual energy which they can use to either bestow a boon or a bane.

Hijras can also come as an invitee to one's home, and their wages can be very high for the services they perform. Supposedly, they can give insight into future events as well bestow blessings for health. Hijras that perform these services can make a very good living if they work for the upper classes.

They are usually rejected for what they are and the way they live. Still, they are tolerated when they show up uninvited at special ceremonies such as births and weddings where they cash in for performing dances and blessings. Avoiding confrontation and the curse of the hijras seems to be the priority for Indians in such circumstances. In any case, they are marginalized and largely left to their own devices to sustain themselves – which include prostitution, dancing, singing and sexual embarrassments of various kinds.

It was not always as such for the hijras. Their presence is recorded far back into India's history. During the time of the Muslim rule before the British, the hijras had a place at court and were generally valued by society. They did not have to resort as much to the sometimes vulgar means of survival they lend themselves to today.

Yet, as a result of their marginalization, a closely-knit subculture has evolved, and in recent years hijras are slowly emerging on the national stage, standing up for their rights.

It is said that globalization plays a huge role in the construction of gender for many cultures in society. Although it may not have struck the attention of many people, globalization affected the gender of the Hijras of India for many years. The Hijras of India are a group of unique and interesting people. The group focuses on beliefs that are extremely different from the beliefs of many other India cultures. Although many people may look down on this group because of their different beliefs and cultural traditions; the Hijras continue what they believe in, and do not care what people have to say. The Hijras' acceptance with their feminine side makes them stand out from everyone else. The Hijras' tradition has been passed on for many generations and continues today. Gender does not play a big role in the Hijras' culture because the Hijras believe that there is no such thing as man or woman. Their focus on doing gender is surprisingly different, but unique. This South Asian society opens the doors for many other cultures by taking chances in what they have always have believed is right. The Hijras make gender non-existence in their society. They believe one is what she wants to be. The Hijras offer a very unique view in the image of a third-gender. The Hijras of today have their ancestors to thank for their traditional beliefs.

The ancestors of past generations offered unique beliefs that set up the modern societies for the Hijras. The concept of making the ancestors proud followed throughout the Hindu belief. If the ancestors were Hijras and still made it to the after world, then the Hijras followed because it must have been promising for life after death.[11] It was nothing but tradition that led the Hijras to making decision that changed the way society views them. This was just a classic example of following tradition and sticking to the beliefs of the great-great-great grandparents. It is up to the Hijras to keep the tradition going. Religion came in with the Hijras belief of gender.

Religion plays a major role in the construction of the Hijras. It is the belief of the Hindu faith that sex is the key to everything. Having sex with this faith is a blessing. The *Kamasutras* are a great way to explain the Hindu beliefs. The *Kamasutras* introduce a third nature which is like the Hijras. It is a man dressed in women clothing giving oral sex to a male customer. Hindu beliefs focus on same sex being normal. When oral sex is being performed with homosexuals it is normal, but once it becomes heterosexual oral sex is a sin.[12] These beliefs show that homosexuality is normal in the society of the Hindus. The Hindu belief led to many dual-gendered figures.

The Hijras believe that dual-gender figures are more powerful the any other identifications. Hijras are men who dress and act like women. They do not consider themselves to be men or women, but a third-gender or sub-cast. They are classified as eunuchs, which are castrated men. The Hijras believe that if they do not go through this type of operation they are worthless, useless, and do not exist. Undergoing this operation classifies the Hijras as being "True" Hijras. This operation is so important because it gives the Hijras the honored right of being addressed in a feminine way with ms, miss, or Mrs.[13] This is a great achievement when the groups of men are addressed with feminine pronouns also because it shows them that they have achieved the honor that generations and generations of Hijras have achieved before them.

Achieving the recognition for a Hijra does not come easy. There are many rituals and ceremonies an uprising Hijra has to go though to become a true Hijra. Many different tribes of the Hijra culture do different types of rituals to be formally accepted into a group that society views as weird. The culture is very different, but necessary to the beliefs of the Hindu. The Hijras are more concerned with being recognized for what they do, rather than what they are. The importance of these tribes are very valuable to society oppose to what many other groups may believe. The Hijras are known throughout many different cultures. Their name carries a value of great importance. The more men engaged in the type of society will bring more people to realize that the Hijras are just another one of them. The Hijras want to be known for the accomplishment of introducing a new gender into the world. Rituals were the great works behind the Hijras.

The rituals of being reborn into a Hijras are widely spreading throughout the Indian culture. The Hijra goes through a ritual in which they are castration. In castration, the men are stripped of all their masculine traits. At these rituals, the men are looked up on as the new upcoming society of the third gender.[14] The Hijra prepare for these rituals as if the ritual was a wedding of some sort. They have to make sure it is the right time of year, climate, and day. Becoming a Hijra is like becoming a doctor or lawyer; might go farther than becoming a doctor or lawyer it is as important as seeing god himself or even their ancestors.[15] The rituals provide the men soon to be Hijras with sight into a better life and future for them. Sexuality is the key to the Hijras' beliefs.

Sexuality is very important to the Hijras. The Hijras are not looked up on as a gendered or sexual, but a great culture born under kinship, religion, class, and hierarchies of respect. When it comes to having sex, there are a great difference between the man who gives the semen throughout intercourse, and the man who receives. The man that penetrates keeps his masculine identity, and the man who gets penetrated is called a queer.[16] The focus of the group is to show who has the power. The belief that many other groups show is if you have intercourse with someone of the same sex, then you are gay or homosexual, but the Hijras belief that if you are parting the all the work into having sex with the same sex then you are not gay. Sex is sex meaning one cannot become gay just because they have sex with the same sex. The Hijras are very straight forward when it comes down to having sex.

Many Hijras engage in sex for many. The man that they have sex with are called their "husbands". Engaging in sex with many men in the community is normal to the Hijra. The main role behind being a Hijra is having sex freely and willingly.[17] Having sex is a type of entertainment for the Hijra. They believe that they could be a good benefit to men as well as the women can. They are not trying to take every husband away from his wife, but they want to single out those men who do not quite know what they are classified as meaning or they heterosexual, homosexual, or third gender. They want to be there for those men who do not feel comfortable saying they are gay, but like to have sex with other men. The Hijras are in the same position as those men. They do not want to be called gay, but they want to be considered the third gender. The roles of the wife and husband change in between the Hijras.

The role of the once men changing in the housing situation, meaning the mother or now fathers and the father (Hijras) are now the mothers. The mothers have to support the families as if she was originally a man. This role is very interesting because the Hijras offer or shows a feminine act by switching roles in the family. The Hijras are looked up on now as mom because he now cooks, cleans, and cares for the children. He now runs the household and keeps everything in order for the family.

Although the Hijras are labeled as a third-gender or sex, they play major roles in the entertainment and celebrations of society. It is more than just being defined as a third-gender, but more as being recognized as a wonder group who made a difference in the world. The Hijras would show up to weddings, birthing, and parties uninvited or unannounced and bless the event by singing, dancing, and drumming. This gathering is not just a celebration, but it is recognition for the Hijra tribe. The celebration gives them a chance to present themselves to society in a way that speaks their beliefs and what they stand for. The Hijras engage in these activities to show that they mean no harm to society, but they only want to be accepted for the good things they do not the type of sexual activities they engage in. The Hijras want society to know that they want to just be looked at as they group that is different and unique in their own way. Health problems are a big issue throughout the Hijras' tribe. The Hijras have many been the concern for many health issues in society and in their community. With the homosexual intercourse the HIV/AIDS virus has spread greatly throughout the community. An issue of human rights and awareness has come up in many government concerns. What to do with men who are intentionally having sex with other men and spreading the HIV/AIDS virus. The HIV/AIDS virus has been sweeping through the Hijra community for many generations, but the Hijras do not really care about the virus because they continue having sexual intercourse with men and spreading the virus.

Society views the Hijras as being nasty, dirty, and a disgrace to mankind, but the Hijras are careless because they have no shame in their belief and culture. The Hijras feel that it is a freedom of choice and sacrifice to engage in something as extraordinary as becoming a Hijra. They think that if they do not follow their ancestors in the tradition then they would be treated badly in the afterlife. It is an honor to the Hijra to have achieved that great name. The Hijras keep their head held high no matter what people in society has to say about their discussion to become this type of gender or group in society. The integration of the Hijras into society has changed the world once known to mankind. At one point the classification of one's gender was male or female, but now there is another gender in the world. This third gender not only roams the areas of India, but all over the continent there are different genders uprising. For instance, in South America there are some Hijras and many other places are seeing the new generation of Hijras. This new addition to society for many places is shocking because what will happen now that there is a third gender.[18]

Some Indian languages such as Sanskrit have three gender options. In November 2009, India agreed to list eunuchs and transgender people as "Others", distinct from male and female in voting rolls, voter identity card, passport etc. [19]

In September 2003, the Peoples' Union for Civil Liberties, Karnataka (PUCL-K) published a truly remarkable report on human rights violations against the transgender community in India. In the spring of 2004, I was fortunate to obtain a hardcopy of the report, and I wish to alert you to it via this webpage.

The 117 page PUCL report begins by providing background on the social, cultural and political context of the Kothis and Hijras. It then documents violence and abuse against these peoples via testimonies of many who have been directly affected, and goes on to discuss the institutional basis of all this violence. The report then documents efforts by the Kothi and Hijra to organize and protest the violence and discrimination that they face. It also documents many useful recommendations on how to improve the plight of transgender people in India. The report concludes with many useful appendices of valuable information, including contact information for Kothi and Hijra support organizations.

The PUCL Report reveals all too clearly the trap that transgender women often fall into in traditional societies: They become outcasts, because they have no family to harbor them, and then - having no means of support - become labeled as a sex object and forced by circumstances into sex work in order to survive. When young and nubile, transgender women may take some degree of comfort in their acceptance as a women by the men who use them sexually, not realizing the long-term difficulties that they will face later in life as they ages in a society that offers no other kind of work for them to engage in (other than begging).

While reading this amazing report, you will be struck with how similar in many ways is the plight of the Hijra to that of young transgender women in many western countries, where so many are similarly forced onto the streets of our big cities. Thrown away by their families, and unable to obtain proper documentation, education and employment, many kids must resort to sex work in violent environments in order to survive.

The life-long social entrapment of many transgender women into sex work in countries like India reinforces the stigmatization of their entire community as outcasts there, creating a veritable caste system of transgender sex workers. The ongoing entrapment of one in every few hundred transgender kids into becoming willing sex objects for the local males thus works to the great advantage of the patriarchal society in which it occurs. However, the women themselves are trapped into a lowly caste from which they cannot escape and which provides them few options for a full and normal life over the long term.

This fate befalls them simply because they are transgender, and thus see becoming a Hijra as being far preferable to the worse fate (to them) of remaining male. Since prostitution is "illegal" in most traditional societies, the police become a state-supported mechanism for enforcing sex worker traditions: The police do not protect the women from abuse, but instead victimize them if they don't keep in line or if they protest the system. As a result, the police are the source of many abuses against transgender women in India, as elsewhere.

After reflecting on these difficulties, the PUCL report has many positive things to offer - especially in its recommendations about how the situation of the Hijra and Kothi can be improved in the future. It also implicitly suggests how very large are the numbers of transgender people worldwide, and how similar are their problems in many other countries.

Sangama[20] is a sexuality minorities human rights organization for individuals oppressed due to their sexual preference. Sexuality minorities include, but are not limited to, hijras, kothis, doubledeckers, jogappas, lesbians, bisexuals, homosexuals, gays, Female-to-male/male-to-female transsexuals and other transgenders. It aim to help live their lives with self-acceptance, self respect and dignity. It especially emphasize the concerns of sexuality minorities from poor and/or non-English speaking backgrounds and sexuality minority sex workers, who otherwise have little to no access to information and resources.

Sangama aims to bring sexuality, sexual preference and gender identity into the realm of public discourse and link it to gender, human rights development and other social movements. It campaign for the changes in the existing laws, which discriminate against sexuality minorities, including sex workers and People Living with HIV/AIDS (PLHA). It work with family members, friends, co-workers and partners of sexuality minorities.

In recent years, police harassment has sharply increased in Bangalore. Blackmail, assault and extortion of money are increasingly being used against sexuality minorities. Public recreational areas (like parks) which were some of the few spaces available for sexuality minorities have become sites of fear. Mainstream society marginalizes, stigmatizes, and encourages this violence. And our legal sanctions legitimize these human rights violations, effectively denying any legal recourse to justice for most sexuality minorities

Sangama actively campaigns for the rights of sexuality minorities to live safe, healthy and empowered lives.

National Campaign for Sexuality Rights(NCSR) is a nationwide campaign working for sexuality rights and the rights of sexuality minorities in India. The campaign is collective effort of groups, movements, individuals and organizations from all over India. At present NCSR has more than 50 organizations as part of its collective process. It raises issues related to sexuality minorities rights issues on different platforms from local to national and international levels (World Social Forum, Karnataka Social Forum, Bangalore Social Forum, International Womens Day, May Day, Human Rights Day, World AIDS Day, National Womens Conference etc.).

Sangama actively campaigns primary focus is on repealing Section 377 of the Indian Penal Code (IPC), which criminalizes adult consensual non-reproductive sexual practices.

Uday Foundation is devoted to systemic change to end shame, secrecy, and unwanted genital surgeries for children born with an anatomy that someone decided is not standard for male or female. In India DSD is primarily a problem of stigma and trauma, not gender Project DSD (Discriminated and Socially Distanced) of Uday Foundation is an education, advocacy, campaigning which works on behalf of people with disorders of sex development following aims:

- To educate, inform and campaign in order to remove the shame, secrecy, social prejudice, ignorance and stigmatization which surround DSD conditions.
- Individual counseling of Parents of New Borns & Children with DSD
- Community awareness projects and campaigns
- Information and referral to specialised medical practitioner or hospital
- Answers to your questions through email.
- Financial assistance in treatment.
- Equal right to education, work and social acceptance.

Hijras are communities of transgender people and people with intersex conditions—mostly men who undergo castration—

prevalent throughout South Asia. Kothis are men who have sex with men and who see themselves as feminine in sexual partnerships.On March 31, 2002, police in Bangalore, India reportedly barred access by human rights activists and community members to a local resource center focusing on sexuality minorities issues, Sangama, for allowing hijras and kothis to meet in its office. Two weeks earlier, police officials entered the office and told employees they cannot allow hijras to meet in the Sangama office—insisting that hijras can only have meetings 'outside Bangalore city.' Activists report additional incidents of police abuse, including arbitrary arrests and torture of those held in custody.

The International Gay and Lesbian Human Rights Commission (IGLHRC) joins Sangama in condemning these reported patterns of police restrictions, harassment, intimidation, and torture directed against hijras and kothis in Bangalore.

It's high time to demand an immediate end to police harassment and abuse against these communities, as well as against those who defend the rights of sexuality minorities in Bangalore and ask for an immediate, sweeping, and fair investigation of previous and current abuses against these communities. Ask the institution of sensitivity training for police officers in Bangalore to discourage discrimination against any group, including sexuality minorities.

Among the millions of new voters in today's Bangladeshi elections will be some 100,000 hijras — cross-dressing, pre-and post-operative transsexuals — allowed to cast ballots for the first time.[21]

The male-to-female transsexuals are among 32 percent of the impoverished nation's 81 million voters for whom participating in the elections, the first since 2001, will be a new experience.

According to Joya Shikder, a Hijra social worker this move spelled a positive change for the conservative Muslim country. They have been overlooked in all previous elections. It's exciting to be given this recognition but the authorities have stopped short of acknowledging them as a third gender. The move to give hijras the vote has been applauded by human rights activities but has caused a headache for Election Commission officials who create separate lines for male and female voters at every polling booth but no line for hijras. According to Shikder, "You cannot just class us into men and women by looking at our faces, bodies and expressions." S. M. Asaduzzaman, Bangladesh Election Commission spokesman informed that officials are still trying to figure out exactly how hijras would cast their votes.

But attitudes are gradually beginning to change.

There are large number of internationally funded support groups that are gaining considerable momentum in many big Indian cities, hijras, as well as other sexuality minority groups, are slowly starting to get a better deal. According to Rex Watts, coordinator of the Bangalore support group 'Sangama', it is necessary to take direct action. For instance, every time a trashy story was published they would ring up the journalist and give them a hard time about it. It has taken time but now they usually go through them before they print something.

Sangama was set up in 1999 and is funded by the Bill Gates Foundation and the Fund for Global Human Rights among others. As well as organising protests and rallies, groups like Sangama have been instrumental in establishing community networks with monthly meetings and safe spaces such as drop-in centres for all sexuality minority groups. Two thirds of their spending goes towards fighting against the spread of HIV infection through awareness programmes and condom distribution. According to Sangama, approximately 18-20 per cent of hijras are HIV positive. According to their report, few years before there were three to four AIDS deaths every month in Bangalore, now there are three to four deaths every year.

Just as successful has been the 24/7 crisis intervention. As soon as someone calls the crisis number nine people immediately rush to the spot. We aim to get all nine people there within 30 minutes. In the areas where they have been implemented, the crisis intervention teams have reduced the cases of police violence against hijras to practically zero. When they are called, to a police station for example, they are straight there, 'Why have you arrested this person? We've been told you beat her?' like this. They still hassle them and take money from them at cruise points, but the violence has stopped.

Vivek Diwan from the Lawyers' Collective argues that attitudes are also changing higher up the legal ladder: "Off the record comments are often made by judges [regarding IPC 377] questioning how this kind of archaic thinking can continue, I overheard one saying only recently, "Get with the times man - there's even a pride parade now in Calcutta!".

Even the Indian government seems to be finally recognising that hijras exist. In March 2000 Shabnam Mausi, or 'Aunt Shabnam' as she is affectionately known, became the first Hijra to be elected into Indian parliament and since then many others have taken her lead by successfully entering the political arena.

In March 2001, hijras were factored into the government's policy-making for the first time when they were named as a target group for a breakthrough de-addiction programme. In the same month the state of Tamil Nadu allowed hijras, if they wish, to be recognised as 'T' rather than just 'M' or 'F' on ration cards with the same being planned soon for passports and driving licences.

This is only a small step for the welfare of this socially deprived group. It should be an eye opener to change the mental psyche that its time not keep them isolate or mock them in the public places, but to accept them as normal beings. One way of solving them, is to through special provision in terms of education, employment and legal opportunities. After all, they are also citizens of the country, deserve every human rights guaranteed by the constitution. Intersex is not a part of the transgender movement. Whereas individuals who are intersexed might identify as transgender, the opposite is not true. Most people who are part of the transgender movement are not intersexed. To include intersex under the umbrella term "transgender," overlooks our specific needs which often are medical reform, legal issues concerning which gender we are, health issues specific to intersexed bodies and more importantly, the fact that most intersexed people are not trans. Many are perfectly happy with being men or women and more and more of us are quite happy being intergender and find the notion of trans totally foreign to our identity because we are rejecting binary gender altogether and the prefix "trans," just like the prefix "bi" mentioned earlier, keeps the binary well intact.

Social inclusion has been a challenge, with which even law struggles at times. Various laws have been quite unsuccessful in changing the dogmatic mind set based on social customary practices. On the other hand, various people including politicians continue to maintain a social status and garner peoples support even after being legally ostracised as criminals. The Section 377, dealing with sodomy, meaning carnal intercourse against the order of nature with any man, woman or animal; is just one sexual aspect of human life. The other aspects of human rights are still neglected. The Indian legal system is still to recognise and protect Eunuchs, the third sex. [22]

Thousands of children born naturally as eunuchs (kinnars or hijras) are pushed out of the so-called mainstream social order. Taken away by the eunuch community, disbanded by natural families due to shame and stigma and socially excluded, the children are left without proper life and development support. Education systems are not sensitive enough to cater to their needs and government is still to ponder on developing support system for such children. Left totally on their own, such children grow to take up similar occupation of begging in a manner of extortion from business persons and families in their times of happiness. This is forced criminalisation of individuals due to social, economic and legal exclusion.

The Indian Constitution is one of the most progressive documents in the world. Under Part III, it deals with fundamental rights of human beings, both citizens and otherwise. Concept of equality and justice are the underlining concept. While emphasising on equality, the Constitution also recognises the need for making special provision for women and children; and also for the advancement of any socially and educationally backward classes of citizens or for the scheduled castes and the scheduled tribes.

The provisions though fail to cater to the need of eunuchs or the third gender but none can deny that they fall in the category of socially and educationally backward class. The need is for Constitutional amendment to include the Hijras so that special provisions can be made including them under the umbrella of state sponsorship, protection and promotion. The fight against injustice and social exclusion is long drawn and has to be dented at the highest level of legal framework. The matter is just not of rights and equality, its much more of equity and justice.

NOTES & REFERENCES

1. http://awonderfuldayforanthropology.wordpress.com\2009\06\29\neither man nor women the hijras of India
2. Nanda, Serena, *Neither Man nor Woman: The Hijras of India*, Belmont, CA; Wadsworth, 1999.
3. Jaffrey, Zia; *The Invisible: A Tale of the Eunuch of India*, New York, Vintage, 1996.
4. "Among thirty of any informants, only one appeared to have been born intersexed"; Serena Nanda, "Deviant careers: the hijra of India" Chapter 7 in Morris Freilich, Douglas Reybeck and Joel S. Savishinsky (eds), Deviance anthropological perspectives (Greenwood publishing, 1991).
5. http://aidssupport.aarogya.com/awareness/269-transgendera_hiv,html sstart=1
6. www.thewe.cc
7. www.saharahouse.org
8. Ravaging the Vulnerable: Abuses Against Persons at High Risk of HIV Infection in Bangladesh, *Human Rights Watch*, August 2003. Report online. See also: Peoples Union of Civil Liberties (Karnataka) Report on Human Rights Violations Against the Transgender Community, released in September 2003. Reported in Being a Eunuch, By Siddarth Narrain, for *Frontline*, 14 October

2003.

9. 'Trans Realities: A Legal Needs Assessment of San Francisco's Transgender Communities', Shannon Minter and Christopher Daley.

10. Associated Press (November 9, 2006). "Indian eunuchs help collect taxes". CNN via Internet Archive.

11. Reddy, Gayatri. 'Men' Who Would Be Kings: Celibacy, Emasculation, and the Re-Production of Hijras in Contemporary Indian Politics. Social Research; Spring2003, Vol. 70 Issue 1, p163-200, 38p. http://search.ebscohost.com/login.aspx?direct=true&db= wdh&AN=9840624&site=ehost-live>

12. Reddy, Gayatri. With Respect to Sex: Negotiating Hijra identity in South India. Chicago: University of Chicago Press, 2005. <http:/ /search.ebscohost.com/login.aspx?direct=true&db= wdh&AN=27452631&site=ehost-live>

13. Reddy, Gayatri. With Respect to Sex: Negotiating Hijra identity in South India. Chicago: University of Chicago Press, 2005. <http:/ /search.ebscohost.com/login.aspx?direct=true&db=wdh&AN= 27452631&site=ehost-live>

14. Arondekar, Anjali. The Voyage Out: Transacting Sex under Globalization. *Feminist Studies*, Summer 2007, Vol. 33 Issue 2, p337-349, 13p. http://search.ebscohost.com/login.aspx?direct= true&db=wdh&AN=27452631&site=ehost-live>

15. Reddy, Gayatri. 'Men' Who Would Be Kings: Celibacy, Emasculation, and the Re-Production of Hijras in Contemporary Indian Politics. Social Research; Spring2003, Vol. 70 Issue 1, p163-200, 38p.http://search.ebscohost.com/login.aspx?direct=true&db= wdh&AN=9840624&site=ehost-live>

16. Arondekar, Anjali. The Voyage Out: Transacting Sex under Globalization. Feminist Studies; Summer2007, Vol. 33 Issue 2, p337-349, 13p. http://search.ebscohost.com/login.aspx?direct=t rue&db=wdh&AN=27452631&site=ehost-live>

17. Arondekar, Anjali. The Voyage Out: Transacting Sex under Globalization. Feminist Studies; Summer2007, Vol. 33 Issue 2, p337-349, 13p. http://search.ebscohost.com/login.aspx?direct= true&db=wdh&AN=27452631&site=ehost-live>

18. http://voicelab9.wordpress.com/non-western-cultural-norms/the-hijras-of-india/
19. Penrose, Walter (2001), Hidden in history: Female Homoeroticism and women of a "Third Nature" in South Asian Part, *Journal of the History of Sexuality* 10.1
20. http://www.sangama.org
21. http://www.taipeitimes.com/News/world/archives/2008/12/29/2003432335
22. http://www.merinews.com/article/third-genders-fight-against-social-exclusion/15774398.shtml

6

Intersex People and Human Rights

There are various legal, social, medical and scientific opinions and theories about what constitutes sex and what constitutes genders. Sex is most easily understood as whether a person is male or female. Some people do not have a sex identity that is exclusively male or female. Gender is a cultural expression of sex identity (often but not always based on stereotypes of masculinity and feminity). Gender can be understood as a person looking, dressing or acting as male or female. Some people's gender identity is not linked to their sex. Despite a lack of consensus over the exact definition of sex and gender, sex and gender identity is an important part of a person's identity according to culture and society, sex and gender identity defines a person's sense of self and positions them in a social and political context. Every person has the rights to have their sex and gender identity recognized and respected. Unlike most minority group, the most tangible discrimination which intersex people have faced been medical. This is partly responsible for why some intersex people organization have remained focused on medical issues as opposed to human rights. But I think many of us believed that the way the medical establishment and others have treated them is unethical and also absurd in its denial of the simple truth that biological sex is not simply 'male' or 'female'.

Global Rights is a human rights advocacy group that works to abolish discrimination based on race, gender, and sexual orientation. I will discuss here some of the rights taken from the report which was originally published as chapter within a larger shadow report focusing on the United States Compliance with the International Covenant for Civil and Political Rights (ICCPR) and was submitted to the Human Rights Committee (HRC) in June 2006. This broader report, in turn, was developed as part of the Global Rights – Coordinated U.S. Shadow Reporting Project: Fighting U.S. Exceptionalism and Demanding Accountability.

This shadow report on lesbian, gay, bisexual, transgender and intersex rights in the United States was coordinated by Global Rights and endorsed[1] by:

- Amnesty International USA
- Gender Public Advocacy Coalition
- Global Rights
- Human Rights Campaign
- Immigration Equality
- International Gay and Lesbian Human Rights Commission
- Lambda Legal Defense & Education Fund, Inc.
- Law and Policy Project, School of Public Health, Columbia University
- National Center for Lesbian Rights
- National Gay and Lesbian Task Force
- Sylvia Rivera Law Project.

This shadow report was originally published as a chapter of the larger shadow report, coordinated by Global Rights *"U.S. Shadow Reporting Project: Fighting U.S. Exceptionalism and Demanding Accountability"* that was submitted to the U.N. Human Rights Committee in June 2006.

Global Rights is pleased to have coordinated this report on the rights of lesbian, gay, bisexual, transgender, and intersex (LGBTI) persons in the United States, in collaboration with ten other U.S.-based human rights and LGBTI rights organizations. Through detailed research and analysis, this report shows that discrimination and violence against LGBTI persons continues apace and makes clear that protecting and promoting the human rights of LGBTI persons must become an urgent priority in the fight against intolerance in the United States. Global Rights is proud to join with other organizations working at the forefront of contemporary struggles for human rights to ensure that the rights of all persons, regardless of their sexual identity, are protected.

Every state party to the ICCPR is required to provide regular submissions to the HRC on their states' compliance with the Convention. Nongovernmental organizations such as Global Rights are then provided an opportunity to submit "shadow reports," in which they offer their own assessments of states' compliance with the treaty. The HRC meets three times each year, in either Geneva or New York, to review these reports, offer concluding observations on states' human rights records, and provide recommendations for actions to improve the protection and promotion of human rights in the those states.

Global Rights is a human rights advocacy group that works to abolish discrimination based on race, gender, and sexual orientation. Our LGBTI Initiative, which oversaw the publication of this report, works with human rights leaders in all regions of the world to prevent, expose, and address abuses directed against individuals because of their real or perceived sexual orientation, gender identity, or gender expression. We believe strongly that international mechanisms, including treaty bodies such as the HRC, provide a useful forum in which human rights advocates may hold governments responsible for domestic human rights violations. As such, they welcomed the opportunity to work with their human rights colleagues to provide a joint assessment of the United States' record with regard to the human rights of lesbian, gay, bisexual, transgender, and intersex persons.

In the United States today, the human rights of lesbian, gay, bisexual, transgender and intersex (LGBTI) Americans are under attack on many fronts. The heady appreciation that marked the decision to abolish sodomy laws in *Lawrence v. Texas*[2] in 2003 has been quickly countered by efforts to enshrine discrimination in municipal ordinances, national legislation, and calls for a Constitutional amendment banning efforts to achieve marriage equality. Discrimination and its accompanying violence continue apace. This report identifies various categories of human rights violations with reference to specific articles of the International Covenant on Civil and Political Rights (ICCPR). At the outset, however, it is crucial to recognize the hostile and often discriminatory landscape that frames all of the cases in this report. Discriminatory animus permeates nearly all categories of human rights violations directed at LGBTI Americans, whether committed by state or non-state actors. Often the discriminatory intent behind other seemingly distinct categories of human rights violation — including deprivations of life, liberty, health, and opportunity — may not be easily or even logically separated from the animus that encourages the violation. It is equally important to recognize that many of the abuses described here are directed at individuals who appear to be transgressing gender stereotypes and the violations themselves often seem intended to "punish" individuals for asserting their right to gender expression.

In considering the first periodic report of the United States in 1995, the Human Rights Committee noted "the serious infringement of private life in some states which classify as a criminal offence sexual relations between adult consenting partners of the same sex carried out in private, and the consequences thereof for their enjoyment of other human rights without discrimination." Since that last periodic examination, the U.S. Supreme Court has significantly altered the legal framework in the United States through its decisions in the cases of *Romer v. Evans*[3] and *Lawrence v. Texas*. The failure of the United States to explain such major legal advances in its most recent periodic report is highly unusual and raises concern that the U.S. government does not fully welcome the gains, nor honor its commitments to enforcing the rights protected in those cases and echoed in the ICCPR.

In *Romer v. Evans*, the U.S. Supreme Court struck down a voter-enacted provision that would have permanently prevented lesbian, gay and bisexual residents of the state of Colorado from claiming anti-discrimination protections under state laws. In the more recent decision of *Lawrence v. Texas*, the U.S. Supreme Court overturned one of its earlier decisions by striking down homosexual sodomy statutes in the United States. The *Lawrence* decision recognized an important link between privacy rights and equality, noting that "[e]quality of treatment and . . . respect for conduct protected by the substantive guarantee of liberty are linked in important respects, and a decision on the latter point advances both interests."

While the U.S. Supreme Court has now invalidated the country's sodomy statutes, the country's criminal justice system has not yet fully embraced the decision. In many circumstances, police authorities and prosecutors continue to make selective use of criminal provisions involving morals offenses to target LGBTI individuals. Although *Lawrence* did not strike down statutes relating to public sexual activity, in some cases the highly selective prosecution of these morals offenses, especially when they involve the mere solicitation of private sexual activity in public places, could intrude on privacy guarantees and limit the impact of the decision. Other discriminatory criminal provisions also seem to have survived after the *Lawrence* decision, raising serious ongoing concerns over the protection afforded to consensual adult sexual activity in the United States.

In addition, the legislative framework for protecting equality in the United States still contains significant gaps that fail to protect non-discrimination rights found in articles 2(1) and 26 of the ICCPR. At the national level, despite years of debate, the United States Congress has yet to pass any version of the Employment Non-discrimination Act (ENDA), which would make it illegal for private employers to discriminate against employees on the basis of their sexual orientation. The bill last received serious consideration in the U.S. Senate Committee on Health, Education, Labor and Pensions in April 2002, when it was recommended to the entire Senate for passage. This leaves employment non-discrimination provisions to the states, but a study by the National Gay and Lesbian Task Force

(NGLTF) estimates that more than half of the population, 52 percent on last count, has no legislative protection against sexual orientation discrimination when seeking private employment opportunities.[4] And many of the existing state-level employment non-discrimination initiatives are also subject to regular challenge and occasional setback. Until standardized non-discrimination protections based on sexual orientation, gender identity, and gender expression are passed into law at the federal level, human rights enforcement in this area will remain highly uneven and arbitrarily subject both to geography and to qualifying employer requirements that differ from state to state, if they exist at all.

The U.S. report also failed to make reference to the limited non-discrimination protections that exist for federal employees and federal job applicants. Unfortunately, the Bush Administration has created roadblocks to these protections and introduced other limitations affecting LGBTI employees within the federal workforce. At least one influential member of the U.S. Congress has accused the Bush Administration of waging a "covert war" on homosexuals in federal employment.[5]

Violence, torture and extra-judicial killings of persons because of their sexual orientation, whether committed by state authorities or non-state actors, raise serious concerns under Articles 6, 7 and 10 of the ICCPR. State acquiescence that results in severe abuse is described extensively in an Amnesty International report, entitled *Stonewalled, Police Abuses and Misconduct Against Lesbian, Gay, Bisexual and Transgender People in the U.S.* The Gender Public Advocacy Coalition's recent report, entitled *50 Under 30 – Race, Class, and Death by Gender,* also specifically documents hate murders committed against individuals who transgress gender barriers, many of whom are underage and belong to non-white communities.

According to the Federal Hate Crimes Statistics Act of 1990, during 2003, the most recent date for which complete data is available, 7,489 hate crime incidents were reported to the FBI by law enforcement agencies. Of those, 1,239 were reportedly motivated by sexual orientation bias, representing approximately 16.5 percent of all reported hate crimes that year. Even though the statistics almost certainly underestimate the total number of hate crimes committed in the country, the proportion of sexual orientation hate crimes as compared to the total number of all other bias motivated crimes is substantial. To date, there is no authority for the federal government to investigate and prosecute hate crimes motivated by sexual orientation or gender identity bias, as it does with hate crimes motivated by other forms of discrimination. While the U.S. House of Representatives voted twice in favor of a fully trans-inclusive hate crimes bill in the fall of 2005, the U.S. Senate has yet to offer support for such an inclusive effort to expand hate crimes protections. As recently as April 2006, an amendment was defeated that could have provided an opportunity for the Senate to consider a hate crimes bill. That leaves protection in the hands of state officials, but NGLTF reports that only 29 states and the District of Columbia have hate crimes statutes that encompass real or perceived sexual orientation, and only seven of those states and the District of Columbia cover gender identity.

The failure of many states and the federal government to add sexual orientation to the categories of bias motivated hate crimes that trigger the provision of additional investigative and prosecutorial resources creates the impression that those crimes are less serious than other bias motivated crimes. This also leaves a significant gap in the protections afforded to LGBTI Americans under Articles 6 and 7 of the ICCPR.

Amnesty International's *Stonewalled* report also investigates sexual, physical, and verbal abuse committed against LGBTI persons in detention. Abuses carried out under these circumstances constitute intersecting violations of ICCPR provisions. In particular, violations of Article 9 are most common when police or custodial officers fail to protect LGBTI persons or deliberately place them in harm's way. Amnesty International has also denounced common police reliance on an individual's "deviance" from stereotypical gender norms as grounds for suspicion or police targeting in a variety of cases.

The compounded impact of discrimination against women because of their sexual orientation requires unique attention, as do various other intersecting forms of discrimination based on race, disability, health status, gender identity, gender expression, and sexual orientation. Within the criminal justice system, for example, lesbian and transgender women face significantly heightened risks of sexual violence from male officers immediately upon arrest and in custodial detention.

The United States generally recognizes asylum claims based on past persecution or likely future persecution as a result of an individual's sexual orientation or gender identity. Nonetheless, U.S. immigration advocates note the difficulty of proving such claims, and the insensitivity of some immigration officials to sexuality-based cases. Asylum applicants must also generally seek protection within one year of arriving in the United States. This short timeline for filing asylum claims can be particularly burdensome for LGBTI asylum applicants who may find it difficult to reconcile the extreme persecution faced in their home communities with the possibility of a more "open" sexual orientation or identity in the United States.

With only a few exceptions, state legislation generally prevents transgender individuals from changing their legal sex unless they have undergone surgery for genital reattribution. In some cases, pre-operative transgender individuals are also prevented from legally changing their names. As reported by Amnesty International, the resulting differences between personal appearance, legal name or identified sex often leads to abuse during police identification procedures.

The "Don't Ask, Don't Tell, Don't Pursue, Don't Harass" policy in the United States is part of a 1993 law prohibiting homosexuals from serving openly in the U.S. military. This constitutes a discriminatory limitation on freedom of expression that was originally intended to loosen restrictions by allowing lesbians, gays, and bisexuals to serve in the military so long as they did not publicly disclose their sexual orientation. The Service members Legal Defense Network, a non-profit organization dedicated to ending discrimination and harassment of military personnel based on their sexual orientation, reports that hundreds of Americans are still discharged every year under this policy.

Surprisingly, in its periodic report, the U.S. government offers as examples of its protection of the right to "expressive association" two controversial decisions of the U.S. Supreme Court in *Boy Scouts of America v. Dale*,[6] and *Hurley v. Irish-American Gay, Lesbian and Bisexual Group of Boston.*[7] In both cases the Supreme Court was required to reconcile freedom of expressive association, which protects the right of individuals to associate freely with those expressing similar political, social, or cultural views, with state prohibitions on discrimination based on sexual orientation. While largely expected, the outcome in each of those decisions still raises serious concerns about the commitment of the United States to non-discrimination rights. It is particularly unfortunate that the U.S. government's periodic report makes reference to the decisions within such a positive context and without a more complete discussion of the complexities of the cases or their impact on LGBTI Americans.

The recently re-introduced amendment to the Constitution of the United States to ban same-sex marriage and similar initiatives that have been proposed and passed in a variety of states are having a significantly detrimental impact on a broad range of human rights protections. The periodic report of the United States mentions the complexities of the marriage debate, but it fails to consider the debate's acrimonious tone, its discriminatory underpinnings, or the potential consequences for the lives of ordinary LGBTI Americans following such a politicized national dialogue. When debate opened on the constitutional amendment in the U.S. Senate in June 2006, Democratic leader Harry Reid noted that "the reason for this debate is to divide our society, to pit one against another."[8] The federal debate also appears to be lending support to state-level initiatives that seek to ban a variety of legal protections for LGBTI Americans and their families.

The uncertainty of the legal status of transgender persons under state law also has a significant impact on family life. As an example, the National Center for Lesbian Rights highlights a 1999 case in which a Texas court invalidated a seven-year marriage between a transgender woman and her deceased husband and refused to recognize a damage award in a medical malpractice case. Discrimination, abuse and misconduct against LGBTI youth remain particularly severe.

Several recent human rights reports have documented the prevalence of verbal, physical, and sexual violence directed at LGBTI youth in schools, in juvenile detention facilities, and in foster care. The government's failure in this context to guarantee adequate protection to LGBTI youth raises serious concern under article 24 of the ICCPR. LGBTI associations in schools have also come under attack. And an increasing number of children are now facing economic challenges due to the government's failure to recognize same-sex relationships involving their parents, or their same-sex de facto step-parents. If a parental figure is unable to establish a legal relationship, a child is often unable to claim health insurance or social security survivor benefits.

As extensively described by Human Rights Watch and Immigration Equality in a recent report, the refusal of the federal government to legally recognize same-sex couples for U.S. immigration purposes also strains the enjoyment of family life, especially with reference to bi-national couples.

The U.S. government should be asked to explain these major gaps in human rights protections when it appears before the United Nation's Human Rights Committee in July 2006.

Articles 2(1) and 26 (Non-discrimination)

The principle of non-discrimination provides a cross-cutting frame of protection for lesbian, gay, bisexual and transgender persons under the ICCPR. In the case of *Toonen v. Australia,*[9] the Human Rights Committee considered the criminalization of private sexual activity between consenting, same-sex adults and found such laws violated Articles 2(1), 17 and 26 of the

Covenant. That decision has been referenced many times by the Committee, by other treaty bodies and by the UN special procedures when affirming that Articles 2(1) and 26 of the Covenant prohibit discrimination based on sexual orientation.

Discriminatory animus permeates nearly all categories of human rights violations directed at lesbian, gay, bisexual, transgender, and intersex individuals, whether committed by state or non-state actors. The Working Group on Arbitrary Detention has recognized, for example, that the arbitrary detention of homosexuals on the grounds of their sexual orientation constitutes a breach of Article 2(1) of ICCPR based on the *Toonen* decision.[10] Similarly, the Special Rapporteur on Torture in his 2001 report specifically noted that "discrimination on grounds of sexual orientation or gender identity may often contribute to the process of the dehumanization of the victim, which is often a necessary condition for torture and ill-treatment to take place."[11] As a result, this chapter references non-discrimination principles under every article of the ICCPR, and in many cases the discriminatory intent behind other seemingly distinct categories of human rights violation — including deprivations of life, liberty, health, and opportunity — may not be easily or even logically separated from the animus that enables the violation.

In considering the first periodic report of the United States in 1995, the Human Rights Committee noted "the serious infringement of private life in some states which classify as a criminal offence sexual relations between adult consenting partners of the same sex carried out in private, and the consequences thereof for their enjoyment of other human rights without discrimination."[12] Since that last periodic examination, the U.S. Supreme Court has significantly altered the legal framework in the United States through its decisions in the 1996 case of *Romer v. Evans*[13] and the 2003 case of *Lawrence v. Texas*.[14] The failure of the United States to explain such major legal advances in its most recent periodic report is highly unusual and raises concern over U.S. government commitments to enforcing the rights protected in those two cases and echoed in the ICCPR.

In *Romer v. Evans*, the U.S. Supreme Court invalidated a voter-approved amendment to the state of Colorado's Constitution that identified lesbians, homosexuals, and bisexuals as a distinct class of persons to be permanently excluded from protections under Colorado's anti-discrimination laws. The U.S. Supreme Court found the sweeping state provision invalid under the federal U.S. Constitution, arguing that under any standard of review it was inexplicable and "born of animosity toward the class of persons affected."

In the more recent decision of *Lawrence v. Texas*, the U.S. Supreme Court overturned one of its earlier decisions[15] by striking down the homosexual sodomy statute of the state of Texas. The Supreme Court found an "emerging awareness that liberty gives substantial protection to adult persons in deciding how to conduct their private lives in matters pertaining to sex." Citing emerging international practice and the European Court of Human Rights, and recognizing that sometimes "laws once thought necessary and proper in fact serve only to oppress," the Court found that its earlier decision "demeans the lives of homosexual persons" and that the Texas statute violated the right to liberty under the Due Process Clause of the U.S. Constitution. As in the *Toonen* case, the U.S. Supreme Court also found a link between privacy rights and equality, noting that "[e]quality of treatment and . . . respect for conduct protected by the substantive guarantee of liberty are linked in important respects, and a decision on the latter point advances both interests."

Despite these two important decisions of the U.S. Supreme Court, the legislative framework for protecting equality in the United States still contains significant gaps that fail to protect rights enshrined in Articles 2 and 26 of the ICCPR. At the national level, despite years of debate, the United States Congress has yet to pass any version of the Employment Nondiscrimination Act (ENDA), which would make it illegal for private employers to discriminate against employees on the basis of their sexual orientation.

The bill last received serious consideration in the U.S. Senate Committee on Health, Education, Labor and Pensions in April 2002, when it was recommended to the entire Senate for passage. This lack of federal protection in the area of employment leaves most lesbian, gay, bisexual, transgender, and intersex (LGBTI) Americans to depend on state or local non-discrimination provisions. At the state level, the Human Rights Campaign reports that it is still legal to fire someone based on sexual orientation in 34 States, while in 44 states it is legal to fire an individual based on gender identity. A study by the National Gay and Lesbian Task Force (NGLTF) estimates that 52 percent of the population has no legislative protection against sexual orientation discrimination when seeking private employment opportunities.[16] According to an interview conducted by the National Center for Lesbian Rights and the Transgender Law Center, 49 percent of respondents reported experiencing discrimination in employment because they were perceived to be transgender. Transgender workers also face discrimination in terms of income, with 64 percent of respondents making less than $25,000 per year.[17]

State-level employment non-discrimination initiatives are also subject to regular challenge and occasional setback. As recently as May 2006, for example, Colorado Governor Bill Owens vetoed a bill that would have prohibited employment discrimination based on sexual orientation, gender identity, or gender expression in the state of Colorado. Conservative advocates in Washington state have tried to add a referendum initiative to the upcoming November ballot to overturn a law passed last year that outlaws discrimination based on sexual orientation in employment, housing, and lending.[18] And several other initiatives to roll-back non-discrimination protections are working their way through state level procedures. In Ohio and Michigan, lawmakers are attempting to bring legal actions against employers who offer domestic-partner benefits to LGBTI workers through challenges that rely on state-level bans to same-sex marriage and related same-sex relationships.[19] Clearly the record of non-discrimination protection at the state level is concerning, at times suggesting the existence of a sporadic campaign to promote discrimination rather than defend against it.

A 2000 report by the U.S. government's General Accounting Office found that even within states, employment non-discrimination coverage for sexual orientation depends on a complex variety of qualifying conditions, including the number of workers employed and the nature of the work, with broad exemptions generally provided for religious institutions and for some non-profit employers.[20] Until standardized non-discrimination protections based on sexual orientation, gender identity, and gender expression are passed into law at the federal level, human rights enforcement in this area will remain highly uneven and arbitrary, subject both to geography and to qualifying employer requirements that differ from state to state if they exist at all. Under current federal employment standards and U.S. domestic practice, the United States remains in violation of Articles 2(1) and 26 of the ICCPR.

While passage of federal anti-discrimination legislation is a priority concern, the NGLTF has, as an interim measure, called for the U.S. Equal Employment Opportunity Commission to record complaints of discrimination based on sexual orientation or gender identity. Such documentation will help establish better statistical data on workplace discrimination. Precedent for such an intermediate step can be found in the federal Hate Crimes Statistics Act. This Act currently requires the Federal Bureau of Investigation (FBI) to record annual data on "hate crimes" that manifest evidence of prejudice based on sexual orientation, even though the FBI lacks corresponding jurisdiction to investigate those crimes and the data itself may only be used for research or statistical purposes.[21] The collection of employment data could also assist the federal government, along with state and federal lawmakers, in assessing the prevalence of LGBTI discrimination within the workforce.

The U.S. report also failed to make reference to limited non-discrimination protections that exist for federal employees and federal job applicants. While there is no explicit statutory provision for these protections, President Clinton issued Executive Order 13087 in 1998 to ban sexual orientation discrimination within all executive branch agencies. For more than five years, the U.S. Office of Special Counsel (OSC) reviewed and took disciplinary actions in cases involving sexual orientation discrimination in the federal workforce.[22]

In February 2004, the Human Rights Campaign and other NGOs found that the OSC had removed references to sexual orientation discrimination from a standard complaint form and from an informational brochure entitled "Your Rights as a Federal Employee."[23] At the same time, Scott Bloch, the head of the OSC, also began questioning his own authority to enforce Executive Order 13087, suggesting the OSC should rely on specific federal statutes to support enforcement actions and that Executive Order 13087 did not provide sufficient legal authority to do so. [24] Advocacy organizations, including the Human Rights Campaign, joined OSC employees in filing a legal complaint, arguing that Bloch was failing to enforce civil service laws and that he was personally engaged in discriminatory employment practices against career OSC employees.[25] After more than a year, the U.S. Office of Personnel Management launched a formal investigation into the complaint in October 2005. No outcome has been announced in the case, and the commitment of the OSC and the Bush Administration to continue taking disciplinary action in cases of sexual orientation discrimination in the federal workforce remains unclear.[26] In the meantime, members of the U.S. Congress have introduced a bill to clarify the previous authority of the OSC to investigate and take action in cases of sexual orientation discrimination in the federal workforce.[27] At least one influential member of the U.S. Congress, Henry Waxman (D-CA), who serves on the House Government Reform Committee, is concerned that the Bush Administration is waging a "covert war" on homosexuals in federal employment.[28]

In a separate case involving the U.S. Department of State, in April 2006 Lambda Legal appealed a lawsuit on behalf of a job applicant who was denied employment as a Foreign Service

Officer. The employment decision was taken because of the State Department's 20-year practice against hiring any HIV-positive employees for the U.S. Foreign Service, including those who are healthy and able to serve.[29] The lawsuit alleges that this employment practice violates the federal Rehabilitation Act, which parallels the Americans with Disabilities Act in prohibiting the federal government from discriminating against people with disabilities.

Article 3 (Equal Rights of Men and Women)

The extent to which sexual orientation is a ground of inequality that uniquely affects women has been considered by the U.N. Special Rapporteur on Violence Against Women. In her January 2005 report, she noted that sexual orientation discrimination, combined with other factors of discrimination, creates "multiple forms of oppression that keep women subordinated." Lesbians, and more generally women who do not live according to the requirements of heterosexist norms, are subjected to violence and rape, as denounced by the Special Rapporteur in many of her reports. The compounded impact of discrimination against women because of their sexual orientation has also been reported by the Special Representative of the Secretary General on the Situation of Human Rights Defenders and in several concluding observations issued by the U.N. Committee on the Elimination of Discrimination Against Women.

One particular area of concern is that lesbian and transgender women face significantly heightened risk of sexual violence from male officers upon arrest and in custodial detention. Amnesty International's *Stonewalled* report of 2005 highlights some examples of typical assaults against lesbians by police officers or guards.[30] The assaults are often sexual in nature. As a common example, a lesbian of color arrested and detained in a police holding cell in Boston was physically assaulted by an officer after having asked him to loosen her handcuffs. The officer reportedly said "You want to act like a man, I'll treat you like a man!" before beating her.[31]

A 2001 publication by Amnesty International entitled *Crimes of Hate, Conspiracy of Silence* reports the case of Robin Lucas, a lesbian who was detained in a facility in California on a first-time, non-violent offense and sent to segregated detention in a men's prison. The male guards harassed and threatened her for being a lesbian and she was raped by three inmates.[32] The same report also describes a case that occurred in Athens, Georgia, in 2004, in which a lesbian was forced at gunpoint into her apartment by an officer and raped. According to the testimony of the woman, the man said he wanted to "teach her a lesson" and that "the world needed at least one less dyke." The perpetrator was brought up on several charges, including rape, but was only found guilty of violating his oath of office.[33]

Many lesbian and transgender women are harassed or sexually assaulted by state and non-state actors for their failure to conform to gender stereotypes. The crimes committed against them often manifest an intent by the perpetrator to "punish" the victim for transgressing gender roles. And when such crimes are committed by police, by prison personnel or by other state actors, or when investigations of these crimes are downgraded, dismissed, or trivialized, they constitute torture under Article 7 of the ICCPR.

Article 6 (Right to Life)

Extrajudicial killings of persons because of their sexual orientation, either by state authorities or non-state actors, as well as deaths in prison that may be attributed to the failure of prison officials to adequately protect LGBTI persons raise serious concerns under Articles 6, 7 and 10 of the ICCPR.

Although there are no recent reports of extrajudicial or summary executions involving federal or state authorities, state acquiescence to private misconduct that results in severe abuse is described extensively in Amnesty International's *Stonewalled* report.

According to the federal Hate Crimes Statistics Act of 1990, as amended in 1994 and 1996, the FBI is required to collect data related to "hate crimes" that are motivated by bias toward race, religion, ethnicity/national origin, disability, or sexual orientation.[34] This data is analyzed in regular annual reports issued by the FBI. During 2003, the most recent date for which complete data is available, 7,489 hate crime incidents were reported to the FBI by law enforcement agencies in 49 states and the District of Columbia. Of those, 1,239 were reportedly motivated by sexual orientation bias, representing approximately 16.5 percent of all reported hate crimes that year. In 2005, the National Coalition of Anti-violence Programs (NCAVP) recorded 1,985 anti-LGBTI incidents (compared to 2,272 in 2004) involving 2,306 victims (compared to 2,617 in 2004). The report published by NCAVP recorded at least 11 murders motivated by the real or perceived sexual orientation or gender identity of the victim in 2005 (compared to 13 in 2004).

While these statistics are almost certainly underestimating the total number of hate crimes committed in the country, the proportion of sexual orientation hate crimes to the total number of all other bias motivated crimes is still substantial. Despite this, the federal government currently lacks the corresponding authority to investigate or prosecute sexual orientation motivated hate crimes, as the U.S. Congress has failed to pass a law that would provide federal jurisdiction to investigate and prosecute the cases if local law enforcement personnel are unable or unwilling to do so. The federal government has authority to investigate and prosecute other categories of hate crimes.

The FBI web site specifically notes that it is required to collect data on hate crimes motivated by sexual orientation bias, but unlike other categories of hate crimes "the FBI does not have federal authority to investigate hate crimes motivated by sexual orientation bias."[35] Moreover the Hate Crimes Statistics Act explicitly and anomalously indicates that nothing in the act "shall be construed, nor shall any funds appropriated to carry out the purpose of the Act be used, to promote or encourage homosexuality." An amendment that could have empowered the federal government to investigate and prosecute hate crimes motivated by sexual orientation bias was defeated in a contentious session of the U.S. Senate in May 2006.[36] As a result, protection is now left to the willingness and legal mandate of state officials.

NGLTF reports that only 29 states and the District of Columbia have hate crimes statutes that cover real or perceived sexual orientation, and only seven of those states and the District of Columbia cover gender identity.[37] In the absence of federal legislation, this leaves a significant gap in the protections afforded to LGBTI Americans under Articles 6 and 7 of the ICCPR. And to the extent that other categories of bias-motivated hate crimes are investigated and prosecuted by the federal government, the failure to provide similar jurisdiction for crimes motivated by a sexual orientation bias also raises serious non-discrimination concerns under the ICCPR.

Reporting and correctly identifying the cases is only the first step. All too commonly, when hate crimes cases are taken up by state or local officials, effective prosecution and subsequent punishment is jeopardized during the legal process. In several notable criminal trials for hate crimes resulting in the death of the victim, defendants have claimed a so-called "gay panic defense." This troubling defense is essentially one of temporary insanity, and it generally involves a male defendant claiming momentary insanity after interacting with someone he perceives to be homosexual or transgender. The defendant often claims that he was animated by fear of a perceived sexual advance. This defense has been effective in mitigating punishments in a number of hate crimes cases, and it appears most effective when jurors manifest similar levels of bias against the victim.[38]

The Gender Public Advocacy Coalition's (GenderPAC) report, entitled *50 Under 30 – Race, Class, and Death by Gender*, focuses on hate murders committed against individuals who transgress gender barriers, many of whom are underage and belong to non-white communities. In these latter cases, serious concerns are raised under Articles 6 and 24 of the ICCPR. For example, the GenderPAC report highlights the case of Gwen Araujo, 17, a Latina-American transgender person, who was killed in October 2002. The victim apparently joined a party with some friends, where she was sexually harassed by one of the girls, and repeatedly choked and hit on the head by some of the boys. While she was still conscious, she was kneed in the head and finally strangled with a rope.[39]

GenderPAC also reports that in June 2001, Fred Martinez, 16, who identified as female, transgender, gay, and "two-spirited" within Native American tradition, was beaten to death in Cortez, Colorado by an 18-year-old youth who then bragged to his friends about having "bug-smashed a homo."[40]

The general failure of authorities to adequately protect basic rights to life and bodily integrity in hate crimes cases also has a strong impact on the way in which domestic violence affects LGBTI individuals. Taken together, excessive intolerance, social stigma, and the lack of legal recognition for most same-sex couples exposes many LGBTI Americans to unacceptably high levels of domestic abuse, including killings perpetrated by family members and occasionally even by same-sex partners. For example, the New York City Gay and Lesbian Anti-Violence Project highlights a particularly violent case in which the dismembered and mutilated body of Steen Fenrich, 19, was found in a park in Queens, New York, the apparent victim of a homophobic murder committed by his stepfather.[41] In April 2003, Adam Bishop, 18, living in the Pittsburgh area, was beaten to death with a hammer by his 15-year-old brother, who then bragged about the attack while referring to his brother as a "faggot."[42]

Article 7 (Freedom from Torture and Cruel, Inhuman, or Degrading Treatment or Punishment)

Worldwide, cases involving violations of Article 7 of the ICCPR have been widely reported by the UN Special Rapporteur on the Question of Torture and Other Cruel, Inhuman or Degrading Treatment or Punishment. In a 2001 report, the Special Rapporteur posits that by failing to conform to rigid gender constructions, sexual minorities worldwide face disproportionate exposure to harassment, humiliation, and rape, violations that are intended to dehumanize the victims, leaving them even more vulnerable to acts of torture and other inhumane, cruel, or degrading treatment. This is certainly reflected in available evidence from the United States.

As noted, the failure of many states and of the federal government to add sexual orientation to the other categories of bias motivated hate crimes that trigger the provision of additional investigative and prosecutorial resources creates the impression that crimes are less serious than other bias motivated crimes. This deficiency means that too few of the crimes are appropriately investigated or prosecuted as bias motivated incidents. This constitutes a failure to protect LGBTI Americans in violation of Article 7 of the ICCPR.

A report by the Human Rights Campaign, entitled *A Chronology of Hate Crimes: 1998- 2002,* lists 651 violent incidents motivated by sexual orientation or gender identity bias that resulted either in death or bodily injury. For example, in February 2001, in Rifle, Colorado, Kyle Skylock, 16, was found unconscious on the side of a road with severe injuries on his head, face, and body. After having left a party in a car with four other teenagers, he was brought to the location at which he was later found, pulled out of the car and beaten for his perceived sexual orientation, reportedly for being a "faggot." No criminal charge has been filed in the case.[43]

In too many cases, police authorities who respond to such crimes may initially side with the perpetrators. For example, in March 2002 in Denver, April Mora, 17, was punched and kicked by three men who carved the words "dyke" and "R.I.P." into her flesh. During the investigation, the police asked the victim whether the wounds were self-inflicted and asked her to take a polygraph test to prove her story.[44] Such hostility from officials investigating and prosecuting hate crimes based on sexual orientation, gender identity or gender expression is common. Amnesty International has a detailed report of a particularly troubling case in which a Cincinnati gay man, 26, was himself arrested even though he was actually the victim of a homophobic crime.[45]

Amnesty International's *Stonewalled* report also investigates and denounces sexual, physical and verbal abuses committed against LGBTI persons in detention. Abuses carried out under these circumstances constitute intersecting violations of ICCPR provisions. Torture and inhuman or degrading treatment committed by police or other custodial agents violate respectively the rights to liberty and security of the person under Article 9 and the right of persons deprived of their liberty to be treated with humanity and dignity under Article 10.

Within this context, it is important to note that the U.N. Special Rapporteur on the Question of Torture has raised serious concerns over numerous cases involving sexual violence in detention facilities in the United States. The U.S. government has responded to those concerns, and the responses themselves provide an overview of the steps the federal government is taking to address patterns of sexual abuse committed with the participation, consent or acquiescence of prison officials in a wide variety of detention facilities.[46] Still, reports by rights groups in the United States suggest the official responses remain insufficient. Specific cases are instructive.

In one of the cases detailed by the Special Rapporteur on the Question of Torture, Frederick Mason, 31, filed a lawsuit against the Chicago Police Department for having been called "faggot ass nigger" and sodomized by two agents in July 2000. The City of Chicago denied the charges, while the two police agents counter-sued on the grounds of malicious prosecution. The Department of Justice's Criminal Section closed the file, claiming the matter lacked prosecutorial merit under federal criminal civil rights statutes.

As also reported by the Special Rapporteur, Kentin Waits filed a lawsuit against the Chicago Police Department for having been physically and verbally harassed with antigay slurs for 22 hours while under arrest. He was awarded limited punitive and compensatory damages in the case.

According to Amnesty International, in October 2003 in Los Angeles, a Native American transgender woman was arrested by two officers on the charge of prostitution, although she told the officers she was only taking a walk. She was handcuffed, hit in the face, insulted with words like "you fucking whore, you fucking faggot," and raped. The paramedics she contacted after the sexual assault refused to believe her story.[47]

Sexual assaults are also common within the context of invasive and painful bodily searches, especially against transgender women. This issue has been extensively reported by Amnesty International. For example, in 2001 in Montgomery, Alabama, a lesbian identified, white, transgender woman was forced to strip naked, dance, and show her penis during a police arrest. She was then subjected to an invasive search of her body cavities, which according to the victim was particularly painful. She was not allowed to see a doctor and was only allowed to shower in the presence of a male guard.[48]

Article 9 (Right to Liberty and Security of Person)

As already detailed, violations of Article 9 have been widely reported in the United States, most often when police or custodial officers fail to protect LGBTI persons or deliberately place them in harm's way. Amnesty International has also denounced cases of "police profiling," which is explained in the *Stonewalled* report as police reliance on an individual's deviance from stereotypical gender norms as a ground for suspicion or police targeting.[49] Selective and discriminatory enforcement of laws and ordinances may also constitute forms of persecution against LGBTI individuals in extreme cases. This practice is reported most often with respect to police harassment of transgender women, with many reports coming from Chicago, New York, and Los Angeles. In many of the cases, the police automatically assume that transgender persons are engaged in prostitution and they may often use trivial excuses to arrest them on prostitution related grounds. In some reported cases from the Transgender Law Center, the possession of more than one condom has been used improperly as evidence to justify the arrest of transgender persons for prostitution. Also, the National Center for Lesbian Rights and the Transgender Law Center have documented cases of sexual touching by police in order to "establish the true gender" of a person, as well as attempts to "shame" transgender women by calling them by their prior names.[50]

Amnesty International reports, for example, that an African-American, transgender woman was stopped by a white, male police officer in New York City while she was leaving a meeting at the Gay and Lesbian Center and was automatically searched for evidence of prostitution.[51] Similarly, in Chicago in February 2004, three gay men who met at a taco stand were stopped, insulted, and threatened with prostitution arrests.[52]

Numerous allegations suggest that police officers also harass transgender individuals on the basis of their gender identity when using public toilets. In one notable case, Dean Spade, a well known transgender lawyer and founder of the Sylvia Rivera Law Project, was arrested in 2002 at Grand Central Station in New York City, together with two friends, for having used the men's room. The charges were dropped as there was no legal basis for their arrests.[53] Many similar cases are regularly reported in New York and elsewhere.

Article 10 (Treatment of Individuals Deprived of their Liberty)

Numerous abuses against LGBTI individuals in detention have been reported by rights organizations. In many of those cases, the abuses are committed by prison or other custodial officers, as already described above with reference to other provisions of the ICCPR. In other cases, guards either fail to prevent abuses by other inmates or place LGBTI detainees in particularly unsafe locations where they are likely to be attacked by other inmates.

In testimony before the National Prison Rape Elimination Commission in August 2005, the National Center for Lesbian Rights denounced the frequency with which lesbian, gay, and bisexual prisoners are at risk of torture, sexual assaults, rape, and ill treatment. For some gay male prisoners, sexual submission or prison prostitution are a means of securing protection from even more violent inmates. In other cases, guards allow attacks on gay prisoners often just by "outing" them to other inmates. In additional testimony delivered at that same hearing before the National Prison Rape Elimination Commission, the National Center for Lesbian Rights also described the case of a young gay man they represent who was placed in a sex offender unit of a state juvenile correctional facility for being gay, even though he had never been accused of a sex offense. Under those circumstances, he experienced three-and-a-half years of sexual and physical abuse. Each time he attempted to defend himself, he was placed in solitary confinement.[54]

In written testimony to the National Prison Rape Elimination Commission, the Sylvia Rivera Law Project also denounced the case of a low-income, transgender woman who was placed in a men's county jail, as almost all transgender women are, and subjected to extreme forms of verbalized sexual harassment and threats from other inmates. She was then inexplicably placed in a cell with a sex offender, where she was raped repeatedly while correction officers ignored her requests for help.[55]

In the report *Family, Unvalued*, Human Rights Watch and Immigration Equality point to a similarly severe case involving a post-operative transsexual woman from the Bahamas who was detained in a New York City Immigration Detention Center in 2003. While facing deportation for not being legally married, she was searched by male guards, insulted because of her gender identity and placed in detention with male inmates for two weeks, where she was constantly harassed. After complaining and being moved to Bergen County Jail, she was first put into a cell with another male detainee and then moved to solitary confinement, where the majority of those detained were sexual offenders.[56]

Article 13 (Expulsion of Aliens)

The U.N. Office of the High Commissioner for Refugees has repeatedly emphasized that persecution based on sexual orientation or gender identity should be considered as grounds for refugee status under the 1951 Convention Relating to the Status of Refugees. Moreover, the application of the principle of *non-refoulement* prevents the United States from deporting individuals to countries where they could be subjected to torture as a result of their sexual orientation, gender identity, or gender expression.

While the case law remains uneven, the United States generally recognizes asylum claims based on past persecution or likely future persecution as a result of an individual's sexual orientation or gender identity. [57] Nonetheless, U.S. immigration advocates note the difficulty of proving such claims and the insensitivity of some immigration officials to sexuality-based cases. Oddly enough, there is also an emerging trend that suggests some immigration officials are arbitrarily denying asylum claims of those who do not subjectively appear "gay enough," or who are perceived as being able to "pass" for heterosexual in the communities they are fleeing.[58]

Asylum applicants must also now seek protection within one year of arriving in the United States, unless they can prove exceptional circumstances and explain why they could not apply within that one-year time limit. This short timeline for filing asylum claims can be particularly burdensome for LGBTI asylum applicants who may find it difficult to overcome their fears of persecution, even in their new surroundings, or to reconcile the extreme persecution they faced in their home communities with the possibility of a more "open" sexual orientation or identity in the United States. Nonetheless, they must make that psychological transition and affirmatively claim specific, identity-based protection as an LGBTI asylum-seeker within one year of their arrival. *Non-refoulement* protections may be claimed at any time, but both the administrative process and the burden of proof are more difficult outside of the affirmative asylum procedure that must generally be initiated within the first year. As a result of these new expedited immigration procedures, there is substantial fear that the United States may be expelling LGBTI aliens in violation of Articles 7 and 13.

Article 17 (Freedom from Arbitrary Interference with Privacy, Family, Home)

As already noted, in the case of *Toonen v. Australia* the Human Rights Committee recognized that adult consensual sexual relationships are covered by the notion of privacy under Article 17. In 2003, the U.S. Supreme Court, in *Lawrence v. Texas,*[59] outlawed the sodomy statutes still in force in many states. However, police authorities and prosecutors have in many circumstances selectively made use of other criminal provisions involving morals offenses to target LGBTI individuals.

The use of undercover police officers to enforce morals regulations, including statutes prohibiting lewd conduct, public obscenity and public indecency, especially against gay men, raises concerns under Articles 2, 9, 17 and 26 of the ICCPR. The *Stonewalled* report by Amnesty International considers the selective use of entrapment schemes to target LGBTI individuals. In November 2004, for example, Alejandro Martinez was arrested for public lewdness in a public restroom at the New York Port Authority for having allegedly responded to an undercover officer who approached him. According to his account of the incident, Martinez repeatedly ignored the undercover officer's advances. The charges were ultimately dismissed and Martinez was awarded compensation.[60]

Solicitation laws are also used selectively to circumvent the decision in *Lawrence* by revitalizing sodomy statutes when same-sex conduct is solicited or committed in public places, such as public toilets.[61] Although *Lawrence* did not strike down statutes relating to public sexual activity, selective prosecutions for these morals offenses could intrude on privacy guarantees and limit the impact of the decision. In a 2005 Virginia case, the Court of Appeals of Virginia upheld a conviction for merely soliciting oral sodomy.[62] These cases raise serious concerns under Article 17 of the ICCPR and the protection it affords for consensual adult sexual activity.

Other discriminatory criminal provisions seemed to have survived after the *Lawrence* decision. It was not until 2005, for example, that the Supreme Court of Kansas overturned a discriminatory provision in the state's so-called "Romeo and Juliet" statute.[63] That law mitigates sanctions for statutory rape charges if the offender is less than 19 years old or less than four years older than the victim, but it only originally applied if the victim and the offender were of the opposite sex. Similar discriminatory provisions apply in other juvenile justice contexts.

With only a few exceptions, state legislation generally prevents transgender individuals from changing their sex unless they have undergone surgery for genital reattribution. In some cases, pre-operative transgender individuals are even prevented from legally changing their names. This places unreasonable burdens on the transgender person, encouraging discriminatory behaviors, especially at the workplace, and intrusion into the person's private life both by state and non-state actors.

The Sylvia Rivera Law Project has been documenting cases of transgender applicants requesting name changes. In one case, where the applicant's request to change first and last names was rejected, a judge of the Civil Court of the City of New York found that there was no legal basis for the court to "appoint themselves the guardians of orthodoxy" with reference to the social tradition of names.[64]

As reported by Amnesty International, the differences between personal appearance, legal name, and identified sex of transgender persons is in many circumstances a cause for abuse by police officers during identification procedures. Often the officers use the birth name or its related pronoun, even if it does not correspond to the gender identity of the person. As a common example, a Latina transgender woman was reportedly arrested in Los Angeles for providing false information when, during a police identification procedure, she identified herself as a woman. The charges in that case were later dropped.[65]

Article 19 (Freedom of Expression)

Violations of the right to freedom of expression related to LGBTI persons have often been reported by the U.N. Special Rapporteur on the Promotion and Protection of the Right to

Freedom of Opinion and Expression. Restrictions and abuses directed against individuals based on their gender expression or related to the expression of their sexual orientation have also been widely reported.

The "Don't Ask, Don't Tell, Don't Pursue, Don't Harass" policy in the United States is part of a 1993 law banning homosexuals from serving openly in the U.S. military. The law fully authorizes the discharge of service members who publicly declare their sexual orientation. As such, it is a discriminatory limitation on freedom of expression that was originally intended to loosen the prohibitions against homosexuals serving in the military by allowing individuals to serve as long as they did not disclose their sexuality. Hundreds of Americans are discharged every year under this policy.

In May 2006, the Service members Legal Defense Network released data showing that the armed forces continued to discharge two lesbian, gay and bisexual military personnel per day in 2005. That discharge rate has been relatively constant in recent years. A total of 742 military personnel were discharged under the "Don't Ask, Don't Tell" ban on openly gay service members in 2005, which is an increase from 668 discharges in 2004.[66]

Article 22 (Freedom of Association)

The U.N. Special Rapporteur on the Promotion and Protection of the Right to Freedom of Opinion and Expression has addressed many cases of violation of the right to freedom of association. The Special Representative of the Secretary-General on Human Rights Defenders has also considered the same issue from another perspective, focusing on how advocates for LGBTI rights are threatened and targeted for violence in several areas of the world.

Surprisingly, in its periodic report, the U.S. Government offers as examples of its protection of the right to "expressive association" two controversial cases from the U.S. Supreme Court in *Boy Scouts of America v. Dale*,[67] and *Hurley v. Irish-American Gay, Lesbian and Bisexual Group of Boston*[68]. In both cases the Court was required to balance freedom of expressive association, which protects the right of individuals to associate freely with those expressing similar political, social or cultural views, with prohibitions against discrimination based on sexual orientation as established by laws in New Jersey and Massachusetts.

The general position of the Supreme Court in freedom of association cases is that the forced inclusion of an unwanted person in a group can infringe on that group's right to define its own membership and express its private viewpoint. As a result, the majority ruled that the Boy Scouts of America could revoke the membership of an openly homosexual scoutmaster and prevent him from participating in the organization. This was a closely divided and emotionally charged decision. As the dissenting opinion in *Dale* recognized, the U.S. Supreme Court had never before found that the right to association in the selection of group members prevailed over state anti-discrimination laws[69]. For that very reason, this decision raises serious non-discrimination concerns, and it is particularly unfortunate that the U.S. government's periodic report cites to it in such a positive context without discussing its impact on LGBTI Americans.

In Hurley v. Irish-American Gay, Lesbian and Bisexual Group of Boston, private organizers of the St Patrick's Day parade in Boston sought to exclude an organization representing lesbian, gay, and bisexual descendents of Irish immigrants from participating in the 1992 and 1993 parades. A Massachusetts trial court and the Supreme Judicial Court of Massachusetts both found the parade was a recreational event that was subject to a Massachusetts state law that prohibits discrimination based on sexual orientation in public accommodation. In a unanimous decision, the U.S. Supreme Court reversed the Massachusetts courts under the freedom of speech provisions of the First Amendment of the U.S. Constitution, noting that the gay Irish organization never argued that the organizers of the parade were acting under color of state authority, and that the gay organization could have sought its own parade permit. The Court found that disapproval of a private speaker's views did not provide sufficient justification for a state to demand a more tolerant message.[70] While not unexpected, the decision raises concerns about the reach of non-discrimination provisions in the United States.

These two decisions of the U.S. Supreme Court reach beyond the right of expressive association and seem to justify private discrimination of LGBTI groups and individuals. Nonetheless, this is a complicated area of U.S. law, and the U.S. Government's periodic report goes on to recognize that in the case of *University of Wisconsin v. Southworth*,[71] the Supreme Court decided that state educational institutions can use mandatory fees to fund organizations whose positions are opposed by particular students provided the financial allocations are decided through a viewpoint-neutral process. This decision has positive implications for LGBTI student groups on public university campuses.

Amnesty International has also documented more common police raids on LGBTI clubs, gatherings and demonstrations.[72] For example, in March 2003, in New York City, a group of LGBTI activists protesting their own exclusion from the St. Patrick's Day parade was reportedly abused both physically and verbally by police, while one lesbian activist was beaten, handcuffed, and dragged head first from a police vehicle.[73]

The failure of the government to protect association rights in local schools is also detailed in a 2001 report by Human Rights Watch, entitled *Hatred in the Hallways*.[74] In many schools, after-school clubs are forming to provide support for LGBTI students and to circulate information on sexual orientation and gender identity within the larger student community. These groups are generally known as "gay-straight alliances." Despite the importance of these clubs both for LGBTI students and for building more tolerant educational institutions, local school administrators have often tried to suppress them. Attempts to ban these associations are sometimes successful, while in other cases school administrators have gone so far as to ban all after-school associations to avoid recognition of a single LGBTI focused group. In other cases, courts have stepped in to protect gay-straight alliances. In Salt Lake City, for example, a judge ruled that the specific prohibition of gay-straight clubs in public secondary schools in the Salt Lake City School District violated federal laws demanding that schools receiving federal funds grant equal access to all non-curricular clubs or associations.[75]

Article 23 (Family Life)

Although the Human Rights Committee in *Joslin v. New Zealand*[76] found that the refusal of a state to open marriage to same-sex couples did not constitute a violation of the scope of Article 23 of the ICCPR, Committee members Lallah and Scheinin argued that the denial to same-sex couples of benefits available to married couples could ground certain discrimination claims under Article 26 of the ICCPR. Later, in *Young v. Australia*[77], the Human Rights Committee found that the lack of recognition of same-sex couples for specific pension benefits, when the government recognized those same benefits for unmarried heterosexual couples, violated Article 26 of the ICCPR and that the distinction constituted an impermissible form of discrimination on the grounds of sexual orientation. Within this context, the *Young* decision by the Human Rights Committee also suggests a definition of family or of a couple that could have implications for the protection of family life under Article 23 of the ICCPR.

Notwithstanding the decision in *Joslin*, the proposed amendment to the Constitution of the United States to ban same-sex marriage, which has been reintroduced in the U.S. Senate, along with analogous initiatives that have been proposed and passed at the state level in a variety of states, could have a broad and significantly detrimental impact on LGBTI Americans. The periodic report mentions the complexities of the marriage debate, but it fails to consider the debate's acrimonious tone, its discriminatory underpinnings or the potential consequences on the lives of ordinary LGBTI Americans following such a politicized national dialogue. When debate opened on the Constitutional amendment in the U.S. Senate in June 2006, Democratic leader Harry Reid noted that "the reason for this debate is to divide our society, to pit one against another."[78]

According to a 2006 report by NCAVP,[79] the highly charged political debate over marriage amendments is impacting LGBTI Americans across the country, with potentially harmful consequences including increased violence, discrimination, and exclusion of individuals based on their gender expression, gender identity, or sexual orientation. The federal debate also appears to be fueling extreme state-level initiatives to ban marriage and a variety of other legal protections for LGBTI Americans and their families.[80]

According to studies carried out by NGLTF and by the General Accounting Office (GAO), marital status provides eligibility for approximately 1,138 federal protections, rights and benefits under at least 1,049 different federal laws.[81] The lack of federal recognition for same-sex couples denies those couples equal treatment under Social Security policies, federal tax laws, immigration laws, and for other major government benefits.[82]

Some states have provided legal recognition of same-sex unions in different forms, from domestic partnerships to full same-sex marriage. So far, however, only the Supreme Court of Massachusetts, in *Goodridge v. Department of Public Health,* has recognized that a state's denial of marriage licenses to same-sex couples creates equal protection and due process concerns under state constitutional provisions. And even same-sex couples married in Massachusetts are denied any of the federal benefits of marriage as a result of the 1996 federal "Defense of Marriage Act" (DOMA).[83] The existence of DOMA makes the U.S. Senate's current debate over a constitutional amendment altogether unnecessary, as the federal government is statutorily prohibited from recognizing same-sex marriages performed in Massachusetts or in any other jurisdiction.

The denial of federal benefits to same-sex couples in the United States raises serious concerns under Articles 23 and 26 of the ICCPR, insofar as the lack of legal recognition prevents same-sex couples from claiming major benefits or services from the government. Appropriate legal recognition need not be in the form of marriage, assuming the same benefits are provided under some other legal status. But the restrictive definition here of the legal notion of family by the U.S. government leads to differences in treatment that contradict the principles of non-discrimination and family life under the Covenant. According to NGLTF, the difference in treatment afforded to wedded couples under federal law is often particularly substantial. For example, the difference in income tax liability between a same-sex couple and a couple that is able to legally marry, where both couples have a combined income of about $50,000, was almost $2,000 per year in 2004, meaning the same-sex couple's tax liability was almost 25 percent higher than the heterosexual couple.[84] Similarly, if same-sex couples were allowed to marry, their Social Security benefits would be higher, and they would be entitled to Social Security survivor benefit and workers' compensation benefits, which they are currently denied.[85] Under the analysis provided by the Human Rights Committee in *Young*, the burden posed by such differential treatment under the country's national pension plan and through the denial of other retirement benefits is impermissible.

As extensively described by Human Rights Watch and Immigration Equality, the refusal of the federal government to recognize same-sex couples also has a burdensome impact on family life under U.S. immigration laws, especially with reference to bi-national couples. The U.S. immigration system is based on a notion of "family reunification," but same-sex couples are prevented from lawfully living together in the United States.[86]

Quoting Human Rights Watch's and Immigration Equality's report *Family, Unvalued* "[i]nternational law recognizes the rights of nations to define their immigration policies. It is nonetheless inconsistent with human rights principles for a state to frame its immigration policies in a way that denies human rights on a basis of proscribed discrimination. When a government allows such discrimination to destroy its own citizens' right to a family life, separating partners at national borders on account of their sexual orientation and HIV status, it strikes intolerably at the idea of equality."[87] Such inequality affects all aspects of the lives and livelihoods of same-sex couples in the United States. Similarly, the restrictive notion of family under U.S. immigration law, which excludes same-sex couples, sends a "devastating message to them about their dignity and worth," as well as "about U.S. society, and what it wants to become."[88] Decisions of the Human Rights Committee have long recognized that immigration deportations may interfere with family life. As such, the lack of recognition and potential deportation from the United States of bi-national couples is alarming. The situation is particularly troubling when same-sex spouses are wedded to U.S. citizens or U.S. residents through legal marriages or other same-sex legal procedures performed in other countries. Such deportations may constitute violations of Article 23,[89] as well as potential violations of Article 13 of the ICCPR. For example, Human Rights Watch and Immigration Equality raise a case of deportation of a British citizen while visiting her American same-sex partner in the United States. Although the couple was living in the United Kingdom at the time and the British partner had never stayed illegally in the United States, she was refused entry to the United States by the Department of Homeland Security, which then launched an investigation into their relationship.[90]

The current federal provision that already defines marriage as the union of a man and a woman (the "Defense of Marriage Act"), as well as the proposed federal and already existing state constitutional amendments that seek to ban same-sex marriage, also frustrate state-level efforts to prevent domestic violence between partners of the same sex. According to the New York City Gay and Lesbian Anti-Violence Project (AVP), bias against same-sex relationships limits domestic violence prevention programs as well as investigations and prosecutions of same-sex domestic violence cases. And efforts to restrict access to the family court system often mean that same-sex couples are denied important protections, including legal mechanisms and mediation services that otherwise regulate family related disputes. Such alienation from the law can escalate tensions in particularly difficult cases, at times even increasing the likelihood of violent outbursts and economically one-sided settlements.[91]

The NCAVP report points to the story of an Ohio woman, 36, who together with her partner of three years and her 16-month-old daughter moved in with the partner's mother. The partner's mother was verbally abusive and bruises and welts soon appeared on the child's body. When the woman tried to flee with her daughter, she was unable to obtain any assistance from the local domestic violence shelter because of the same-sex nature of her relationship with her partner.[92]

According to Amnesty International, the poor response of police authorities in domestic violence cases involving two partners of the same sex is often alarming. For example, in 2002, in Washington, D.C., a transgender woman who was choked by her male partner was later arrested and charged with assaulting her abuser.[93] The uncertainty of the legal status of transgender individuals under state law also has a significant impact on their family life. As the National Center for Lesbian Rights explains, in those states that do not legally recognize sex reassignment, paradoxically, de facto same-sex unions between a post-operative transsexual and a spouse (the opposite-sex partner at the time of the celebration of the marriage) are legal, while opposite-sex marriage between a transsexual and a partner of the opposite sex may be invalidated.

The state's ambivalence in recognizing the legal effects of marriages involving transsexual individuals may also constitute a serious violation of Article 23 of the ICCPR.[94] For example, the National Center for Lesbian Rights highlights a 1999 case in which a Texas court invalidated a seven-year marriage between Christine Littleton, a transgender woman, and her deceased husband, and refused to recognize damage compensation awarded for her husband's death in a medical malpractice case.[95]

Article 24 (Special Protection of Children)

Discrimination, abuse, and misconduct against LGBTI youth raise additional crosscutting issues that may be linked to multiple violations of the provisions of the ICCPR. LGBTI teenagers are particularly vulnerable to hate crimes, as highlighted in Gender PAC's report,*50 Under 30 – Race, Class, and death by Gender*. And the government's failure to guarantee adequate protections for LGBTI youth in school, foster care, and juvenile detention also raises serious concern.

LGBTI teenagers are especially vulnerable to domestic violence. According to a 2004 report by NCAVP, domestic violence has increased significantly in recent years for the lower age groups tracked by the organization's statistics. And within that group, teenagers are particularly vulnerable to physical and verbal violence when they disclose their sexual orientation or gender identity to their families. As indicated by the National Center for Lesbian Rights and the Transgender Law Center, domestic violence is extremely common against children who begin to express a gender that is different from the one assigned at birth, and parents sometimes subject their children to harmful "mental health" practices in such cases.[96]

Physical, verbal, and sexual abuse against underage LGBTI individuals is also common within juvenile correctional facilities. Testimony by the National Center for Lesbian Rights before the National Prison Rape Elimination Commission raised the case of a 17- year-old gay boy in a Louisiana facility who was regularly forced to have sex with 10 other juvenile inmates. He was forcibly raped at least four times, and the staff of the facility constantly refused his requests to be placed in protective custody.[97] According to testimony, staff at the facility assumed that because the youth was gay, he desired sexual activity and so refused to intervene even when requested to do so. When staff in juvenile facilities do intervene in sexual violence cases, at-risk LGBTI youth are often placed in extended isolation for their own protection.[98]

The problem of harassment and violence against LGBTI

teenagers is also commonplace in schools. According to a 2005 report of the Gay, Lesbian and Straight Education Network, 33 percent of teens reported that students in their schools were harassed because of their real or perceived sexual orientation, while 52 percent of all students personally overheard other students making homophobic remarks.[99] LGBTI students are three times as likely as other students to feel unsafe at school, and 90 percent of LGBTI students report having been verbally or physically abused at school.[100]

Human Rights Watch also documented abuses in schools in its 2001 report *Hatred in the Hallways.* That report highlights a 1996 case brought by a Wisconsin student who was verbally and physically assaulted from middle-school onward. The details of the case are shocking. The student was sexually humiliated, beaten, and urinated on, and he sustained internal injuries on at least one occasion. He attempted suicide twice. The school district was ultimately held responsible for the abuse, since the school principal failed to intervene even though she was aware of the violence. While the details of that case were especially alarming, the patterns of abuse in the case are not unusual. Lesbian teenagers are particular targets of sexual harassment. A 2002 report by NGLTF provides accounts of eight "gang rape" incidents involving 11 students, some as young as sixth grade. In one case, a lesbian teenager who had been harassed for a sustained period of time was severely beaten and raped by a group of students who wanted to teach her to "stay away from their girls."[101]

The National Coalition of Anti-Violence Programs details the case of a 13-year-old boy with developmental disabilities who was verbally and physically harassed in a small Catholic middle-school because of his perceived sexual orientation. Despite his mother's reports, the principal did not intervene in the case.[102] The lack of intervention by teachers and administrators in school violence cases involving LGBTI youth was also widely reported by Human Rights Watch in its 2001 report on the subject.

According to another study by the Human Rights Campaign, children are also discriminated against and face unique economic challenges because of the failure of the government to recognize same-sex relationships involving their parents, or their same sex de facto step-parents. If a parental figure is unable to establish a legal relationship, the child may not be entitled to health insurance or to Social Security survivor benefits. Same-sex parenting is becoming more common, so these legal prohibitions are also becoming increasingly harmful to the special protection of children.

According to the Williams Institute at UCLA Law School, up to 40 percent of same-sex couples aged 22 to 55 years old are raising children, and about five percent of those children are adopted. Unfortunately, same-sex parents face a wide variety of legal obstacles, including a state-level ban on gay adoptions in Florida and significant obstacles to the recognition of same-sex adoptions in many other states. In *Lofton v. Secretary of Department of Children and Family Services*, the U.S. Eleventh Circuit Court of Appeals upheld Florida's adoption ban in a 2004 case, finding the ban "rationally related to Florida's interest in furthering the best interests of adopted children by placing them in families with married mothers and fathers."[103] Some states even prohibit LGBTI Americans from serving as foster parents. In addition, LGBTI employees must often pay from their own salary to receive domestic benefits for their same-sex partners or their partners' children, while married heterosexual employees in the same situation are more often exempt from such payments.[104] Even when health and other benefits for same-sex partners and their children are provided by employers, that support is treated as a taxable benefit to the employee. The Human Rights Campaign notes that similar benefits are not taxed by the federal government when provided to married heterosexual couples.[105]

While the U.S. Supreme Court has now invalidated the country's sodomy statutes and recognized a right to sexual privacy, the country's criminal justice system has not yet fully embraced the contours of that decision. Police authorities and public prosecutors must not turn to selective criminal prosecutions for morals offenses to limit protections for consensual adult sexual activity that are now recognized in the United States. Standardized non-discrimination protections based on sexual orientation, gender identity, and gender expression should be passed into law at the federal level, especially in the area of employment non-discrimination. While passage of federal anti-discrimination legislation covering sexual orientation, gender identity, and gender expression in the workplace remains a priority, as an immediate interim measure, the federal government should begin to record workplace complaints involving such discrimination. The effort will help establish better statistical data on employment discrimination and may lead to more effective protection and legislation in the workplace. Non-discrimination protections that exist for federal employees and federal job applicants should be reaffirmed by the U.S. president, and executive officers must be instructed to enforce them. Other health and employment related limitations affecting LGBTI employees within the federal workforce should be rescinded.

The federal government should add sexual orientation to the list of bias-motivated hate crime categories that trigger the provision of additional investigative and prosecutorial resources from the FBI and other government offices. The failure to do so leaves the impression that such crimes are less serious than other bias motivated crimes, and it also leaves a significant gap in the protections afforded to LGBTI Americans under Articles 6 and 7 of the ICCPR. Reports of UN Special Rapporteurs raise serious concerns over violations of article 9 of the Covenant, especially in situations where police or prison administrators fail to protect LGBTI persons or deliberately place them in harm's way. The United States must take greater care to protect the rights of LGBTI prisoners. The United States must also take steps to prevent the selective and inappropriate arrest, harassment, and prosecution of individuals who transgress stereotypical gender norms, since those individuals are also more vulnerable to abuse and torture in detention.

The compounded impact of discrimination against women because of their sexual orientation requires additional attention and documentation in subsequent reports, as do other intersecting forms of discrimination based on race, disability, health status, gender identity, gender expression, and sexual orientation. Immigration officials should receive additional sensitivity training to assist in the adjudication of asylum and other immigration claims based on sexual orientation, gender identity, or gender expression. Additional protections should also be considered for asylum applicants who must generally seek protection within one year of arriving in the United States, since such a short timeline for filing asylum claims can be particularly difficult for LGBTI applicants.

State laws should be streamlined to facilitate applications from both pre-operative and post-operative transgender individuals who wish to change their names or legal sex on official documents. Current barriers to such identity changes place transgender persons at greater levels of risk during police questioning and identification procedures. The uncertain legal status of transgender persons under state law also has a significant impact on family life that must be clarified by the federal government.

The "Don't Ask, Don't Tell, Don't Pursue, Don't Harass" policy in the United States constitutes a discriminatory limitation on freedom of expression and should be rescinded. LGBTI Americans should be allowed to serve openly in the U.S. Armed Forces. The federal government must recognize that the recently re-introduced amendment to the Constitution of the United States to ban same-sex marriage is having a detrimental impact on a broad range of human rights protections. The denial of rights and benefits to same-sex couples unreasonably burdens LGBTI Americans and raises substantive consequences under the principles of non-discrimination and family life as established by Articles 2(1), 23 and 26 of the ICCPR. The United States should repeal the Defense of Marriage Act and provide appropriate legal recognition for same-sex couples and their families at the federal level. Widespread discrimination and abuse against LGBTI youth pose significant human rights concerns. Current levels of verbal, physical, and sexual violence directed at LGBTI youth in schools, juvenile detention facilities, and foster care are legally unacceptable under the Covenant. The United States must take immediate steps to protect LGBTI youth from all forms of violence. The refusal of the federal government of recognize same-sex couples for U.S. immigration purposes strains the enjoyment of family life, especially with reference to binational couples, and leads to serious violations of the Covenant.

So, it is clear that there is no separate right treaty focusing on sexuality and gender rights but LGBTI people have the right to enjoy all human rights available to other members of the community. In particular, people who are LGBTI enjoy the fundamental rights of non-discrimination and equality before the law. The United Nations Human rights Committee has been very clear that the principle of non-discrimination and equality before the law protect LGBTI people under international law. The non-discrimination provisions are in the International Covenant on Civil and Political Rights (ICCPR), the International Covenant on Economic, Social and Cultural Rights (ICESCR), the Convention on the Rights of the Child (CRC), the International Convention on the Elimination of All Forms of Racial Discrimination (CERD) and Convention on the Elimination of All Forms of Discrimination Against women. As we have seen that Article 2 of the ICCPR sets out the principle of non-discrimination: East State party to the present covenant undertakes to respect and ensure to all individuals within its territory and subject to its jurisdiction the rights recognized in the present covenant, without distinction of any kind such as race, colours, sex, language, religion, political or other opinion, national or social origin, property, birth or other status. Article 26 of the ICCPR sets out the principle of equality. All persons are equal before the law and are entitled without any discrimination to the equal protection of the law. In this respect, the law shall prohibit any discrimination and guarantee to all person equal and effective protection against discrimination of any ground such as race, colours, sex, language, religion, political or other opinion, national or social origin, property, birth or other status. In March 2007, a group of human rights experts developed and adopted what is known as the Yogyakarta Principle. The Yogyakarta Principle confirm that all international human rights laws apply to LGBTI people.

Organisational Intersex International (OII) is the largest intersex organisation in the world. OII membership is mostly made up of intersex people. OII was formed in 1997 by Curtis Hinkle, with the support of some intersex friends, in reaction to the limited voice intersex people had. OII has few policies (opposition to non-consensual infant surgery are among those who do have) and is an affiliation of intersex people (95%) and their friends.

Curtis established OII after fighting a discrimination case in the US and finding little support for intersex rights there. Those organisations that did exist were either ineffective or selective. Some had a policy of discrimination, considering some differences not intersex or not intersex enough. Others required proof, such as a letter from a doctor or some other kind of medical record to establish intersex credentials.

OII decided that anyone who was "game" enough to call themselves intersex was most likely intersex. There are those that claim some transsexual and transgender individuals claim intersex as a way of excusing their apparent change of sex.

OII considers this a ludicrous notion given the far greater disrespect, ignorance, and lack of appropriate medical services intersex people have, and that is not to diminish the enormous discrimination against transsexuals.

OII Australia considers the idea of intersex "privilege" as fundamentally transphobic. OII provides support for intersex people through the provision of information, advocating for intersex rights, attempting to change medical paradigms so that appropriate medical services are available for their diverse needs. OII Australia was established with Hinkle's encouragement, with the aim of providing support for Intersex in Australasia, and specifically to bring about legislative change that would see intersex people given the same rights and freedoms that are enjoyed by most other Australians. OII Australia's specific objectives are in Australian federal and state laws. However, they support OII international affiliates in efforts to have intersex rights recognized worldwide.

OII would rather fight for equal treatment of all human beings so that intersex difference was insignificant in terms of human rights. Because of the gender binary structure within western social paradigms, they have to struggle against basic ideas of what constitutes a human being before we even begin to explain their predicament.

There should be no need for women to have to fight for equality, just as there should be no need for a person of any race or religion to have to fight for it. If all people were guaranteed equal rights, OII would be a social group and little else.

Unfortunately they are constrained to work with what they have, so salami tactics are the only option: that is to fight for each right law by law, one at a time.

Intersex challenges the notion of what is a man and what is a woman. The marriage act defines marriage as a relationship "between a man and a woman". They say the act should therefore define "man" and "woman", and they also maintain that this is impossible to say with any precision. OII Australia's position is that the current marriage act excludes intersex individuals from marriage, and that any intersex person who is currently married is only able to be so because of a pretence that they are wholly man or woman. They believe that if same-sex marriages are allowed, they will be no better off because even that relies on a male/female gender binary.

OII Australia works for the right of all to marry, irrespective of difference — sex or otherwise. The new status would be equally recognized legally with the male and female gender, and it would enable people to change their gender on passports and driving licences even if they do not undergo surgery.But for transgender lobby groups, "intersex" is not a term that they are satisfied with and are demanding a fourth legal gender called "other", which is for people who feel they do not fit into any gender.The proposals listed in a discussion paper are quietly being issued to transgender and transsexual advocates by the commission, a statutory body that advises the Government on such matters. The paper is entitled "Sex Files - The legal recognition of sex: Proposed reform", with the new "intersex" gender listed as a "key feature of the reform proposal being developed by the commission". "Recognition of intersex: Persons who cannot or do not identify as either male or female would be able to choose to be identified on their birth certificate and passport as intersex," it stated. "A person who cannot or chooses not to undergo surgery would not be automatically ineligible to request a change in their legal sex," it said. A response to the report by Sex and Gender Education Australia says there needs to be a fourth legal gender for people who are not even "intersex".

SAGE spokeswoman Tracie O'Keefe, a sexologist whose doctorate comes from a Californian hypnotherapy institute, and who is the co-author of the book 'Transpeople in Love', feels that a fourth gender would be good. The AHRC proposal does not go far enough in providing legal status and social spaces by only allowing people to be male, female and intersex," News.com.au quoted her as saying. Dr O'Keefe, who runs the Australian Health and Education Centre and the International Sex, Gender and Sexuality Clinic in Glebe, said cultures such as Native Americans had more than two genders.

I would like to wind up this chapter by writing that the autonomy and right to self determination of the person with an intersex condition is violated by the surgeries are done without truly consent; parents are often not told the failure rate of, lack of evidentiary support for, and alternatives to surgery. Social distress is a reason to change society, not the bodies of children. Social acceptance of human diversity and an end to the idea that difference equal disease. By contrast, as in the women's right's movement, the civil rights movement, and the LGBT rights movements, the goal of intersex advocacy group is to have people understand intersex condition as a human rights issue.

NOTES & REFERENCES

1. The UCLA Williams Institute also contributed to the report.
2. 539 U.S. 558 (2003)
3. 517 U.S. 620 (1996).
4. National Gay and Lesbian Task Force, Press Release of January 27, 2006; see also, "Legislating Equality," by Wayne van der Meide for the Policy Institute of the National Gay and Lesbian Task Force.
5. See Federal EEO Advisor, Vol. 9, No. 3, April 1, 2006 (quoting Rep. Waxman); Rep. Waxman has also introduced a bill in the U.S. Congress, H.R. 3128, to protect gay federal employees.
6. 530 U.S. 640 (2000).
7. 515 U.S. 557 (1995).
8. "Senators Debate Gay Marriage Ban," June 6, 2006, *The Washington Post,* at A3.
9. Communication no. 488/1992
10. See Reports of December 16, 2002 and December 15, 2003, as well as the opinion on Egypt adopted January 24, 2003.
11. UN Special Rapporteur on Torture, Interim Report to the General Assembly (July 2001, A/56/156).
12. U.N. Doc. CCPR/C/79/Add.50 at para. 287 (1995).
13. 517 U.S. 620 (1996).
14. 539 U.S. 558 (2003).
15. Overturning Bowers v. Hardwick, 478 U.S. 186 (1986).
16. National Gay and Lesbian Task Force, Press Release of January 27, 2006; see also, "Legislating Equality," by Wayne van der Meide for the Policy Institute of the National Gay and Lesbian Task Force.
17. National Center for Lesbian Rights, Transgender Law Center, Trans Realities (2003) at http://www.nclrights.org/publications/transrealities0803.htm

18. "Eyman to File Signatures to Repeal Gay Rights Law," June 1, 2006, *Seattle Post-Intelligencer.*

19. See "An Unequal World," *The Economist,* May 20, 2006.

20. Sexual-Orientation-Based Employment Discrimination, GAO/OGC-00-27R.

21. 28 USC § 534; see also discussion, infra, under Article 6.

22. The OSC recognizes itself as "an independent investigative and prosecutorial agency. Its primary mission is to safeguard the merit system in federal employment by protecting federal employees and applicants from prohibited personnel practices."

23. Human Rights Campaign, Press Release, February 13, 2004.

24. Legal Interpretation of Discrimination Statute, U.S. Office of Special Counsel Press Release, PR04-01, available at http://www.osc.gov/documents/press/2004/pr04_01.htm.

25. See "Special Counsel's Chief is Assailed; Bloch Accused of Silencing Staff," *The Washington Post,* April 16, 2004 at A19.

26. In January 2006 the Government Accountability Office, an independent investigative agency that reports to the U.S.Congress, recommended that an outside organization should review all such personnel allegations against Office of Special Counsel employees. See U.S. Office of Special Counsel - *Selected Contracting and Human Capital Issues,* GAO-06-16.

27. H.R. 3128, introduced June 30, 2005 by Rep. Waxman and Rep. Shays

28. Federal EEO Advisor, Vol. 9, No. 3, April 1, 2006; Rep. Waxman has introduced a bill in the U.S. Congress, H.R.3128, to protect gay federal employees.

29. Taylor v. Rice, Case No. 05-5257, United States Court of Appeals for the District of Columbia Circuit.

30. Amnesty International, Stonewalled, Police abuses and misconduct against lesbian, gay, bisexual and transgenderpeople in the U.S. (2005)

31. Amnesty International, Stonewalled, *Police abuses and misconduct against lesbian, gay, bisexual and transgender people in the U.S.* (2005), at 64.

32. Amnesty International, *Crimes of Hate, Conspiracy of Silence* (2001), at 30
33. Amnesty International, Stonewalled, Police abuses and misconduct against lesbian, gay, bisexual and transgender people in the U.S. (2005), at 41.
34. 28 USC § 534
35. http://miami.fbi.gov/hate.htm.
36. See Lou Chibbaro, "Hate Crimes Bill Dies in the Senate," *Washington Blade*, May 8, 2006, available at http://www.washingtonblade.com/2006/5-11/news/national/killbill.cfm
37. At http://www.thetaskforce.org/theissues/issue.cfm?issueID=12
38. See recommendation of National Coalition of Anti-violence Programs, Anti-lesbian, gay, bisexual and transgender violence in 2005 (2006), at 12 (noting the extent to which the "gay panic defense" is considered a serious problem in criminal trials and recognizing that the California Assembly has introduced a bill to limit the use of this legal defense in criminal trials in California).
39. GenderPAC, 50 Under 30 – Race, Class, and death by Gender (2006), at 4
40. GenderPAC, 50 Under 30 – Race, Class, and death by Gender (2006), at 10
41. New York City Gay and Lesbian Anti-Violence Project, New York Lesbian, Gay, Transgender and Bisexual Domestic Violence Report (2005), at 5.
42. National Coalition of Anti-violence Programs, LGBT domestic violence in 2003 (2004), at 6.
43. Human Rights Campaign, *A Chronology of Hate Crimes: 1998-2002* (2003), at 27
44. Human Rights Campaign, *A Chronology of Hate Crimes: 1998-2002* (2003), at 49
45. Amnesty International, Stonewalled, *Police abuses and misconduct against lesbian, gay, bisexual and transgender people in the U.S.* (2005), at 78
46. E/CN.4/2005/62/Add. 1, at paras 1864-1869 (March 30, 2005).
47. Amnesty International, Stonewalled, *Police abuses and*

misconduct against lesbian, gay, bisexual and transgender people in the U.S. (2005), at 40

48. Amnesty International, Stonewalled, *Police abuses and misconduct against lesbian, gay, bisexual and transgender people in the U.S.* (2005), at 41.

49. Amnesty International, Stonewalled, *Police abuses and misconduct against lesbian, gay, bisexual and transgender people in the U.S.* (2005), at 13

50. National Center for Lesbian Rights, Transgender Law Center, Trans Realities (2003) at http://www.nclrights.org/publications/transrealities0803.htm

51. Amnesty International, Stonewalled, *Police abuses and misconduct against lesbian, gay, bisexual and transgender people in the U.S.* (2005), at 16-17

52. Amnesty International, Stonewalled, *Police abuses and misconduct against lesbian, gay, bisexual and transgender people in the U.S.* (2005), at 16-17

53. Amnesty International, Stonewalled, *Police abuses and misconduct against lesbian, gay, bisexual and transgender people in the U.S.* (2005), at 20; Sylvia Rivera Law Project, at http://www. srlp.org/index.php?sec=03C&page=genderseg

54. National Center for Lesbian Rights, Testimonies submitted to the National Prison Rape Elimination Commission on August 15th 2005, available at http://www.nclrights.org/releases/prison_testimony_081905.htm

55. Sylvia Rivera Law Project, Testimony of Z Arkles (2005), athttp://www. srlp.org/index.php?sec=03N&page=criminaljust

56. Human Rights Watch & Immigration Equality, Family, Unvalued (2006), at 85-86

57. Such cases have been fully recognized since June 1994, when the Toboso-Alfonso case, 20 I&N Dec. 819 (BIA 1990), was adopted as precedent for all future cases.

58. See Punishing Masculinity in Gay Asylum Claims, 114 Yale L.J. 913 (2005)

59. 539 U.S. 558 (2003)

60. Amnesty International, Stonewalled, Police abuses and

misconduct against lesbian, gay, bisexual and transgender people in the U.S. (2005), at 25

61. See opening brief on appeal filed in the Court of Appeals in Virginia submitted by Lambda Legal at http://www.lambdalegal.org/cgi-bin/iowa/cases/brief.html?record=1755

62. Singson v. Virginia, 46 Va. App. 724; 621 S.E.2d 682 (2005)

63. Kansas v. Limon, 280 Kan. 275; 122 P.3d 22 (2005).

64. Civil Court of the City of New York, County of New York, In the Matter of the application of Frank Joseph Guido, Jr., decision of October 24, 2003; see also the Petitioner's memorandum of law in support of Petition for individual adult change of name drafted by Dean Spade, Esq., Sylvia Rivera Law Project

65. Amnesty International, Stonewalled, *Police abuses and misconduct against lesbian, gay, bisexual and transgender people in the U.S.* (2005), at 18-19

66. Servicemembers Legal Defense Network, Press Release of May 24, 2006, available at:http://www.sldn.org/templates/press/record.html?record=2979

67. 530 U.S. 640 (2000)

68. 515 U.S. 557 (1995)

69. Dale, 530 U.S. 640, 679 (dissenting opinion of Justices Stevens, Souter, Ginsburg and Breyer)

70. Hurley, 515 U.S. 557, 581

71. 529 U.S. 217 (2000)

72. Amnesty International, Stonewalled, *Police abuses and misconduct against lesbian, gay, bisexual and transgender people in the U.S.* (2005), at 30

73. Amnesty International, Stonewalled, *Police abuses and misconduct against lesbian, gay, bisexual and transgender people in the U.S.* (2005), at 31

74. Human Rights Watch, Hatred in the Hallways (2001)

75. East High Gay/Straight Alliance v. Board of Education of Salt Lake City School District, 81 F. Supp. 2d 1166, 1197 (D. Utah 1999)

76. Communication No. 902/1999

77. Communication No. 941/2000
78. "Senators Debate Gay Marriage Ban," June 6, 2006, The Washington Post, at A3
79. National Coalition of Anti-violence Programs, Anti-lesbian, gay, bisexual and transgender violence in 2005 (2006), at 17
80. In February 2006, the U.S. Court of Appeals for the Eighth Circuit heard arguments in a case challenging an extreme antigay family law in Nebraska that bans all protections for the relationships of same-sex couples. Citizens for Equal Protection, Inc., et al v. Attorney General Jon Bruning, et al, filed in the U.S. Court of Appeals for the 8th Circuit, case number 05-2604. Legal documents are available at www.aclu.org/caseprofiles and www.lambdalegal.org
81. United States General Accounting Office, GAO/OGC-97-16, January 13, 1997; see also the National Gay and Lesbian Task Force discussion at http://www.thetaskforce.org/theissues/issue.cfm?issueID=14
82. National Gay and Lesbian Task Force, Economic Benefits of Marriage under Federal and Oregon Law (2004), at 4
83. Pub. L. No. 104-199, 100 Stat. 2419 (Sept. 21, 1996), 1 U.S.C. § 7 and 28 U.S.C. § 1738C
84. National Gay and Lesbian Task Force, Economic Benefits of Marriage under Federal and Oregon Law (2004), at 5
85. National Gay and Lesbian Task Force, Economic Benefits of Marriage under Federal and Oregon Law (2004), at 4-11; National Lesbian and Gay Task Force, *Economic Benefits of Marriage under Federal and Connecticut Law* (2005)
86. Human Rights Watch & Immigration Equality, Family, Unvalued (2006), at 35
87. Human Rights Watch & Immigration Equality, Family, Unvalued (2006), at 129-130
88. Human Rights Watch & Immigration Equality, Family, Unvalued (2006), at 138
89. L. Ayoub, S. Wong, Separated and Unequal, *William Mitchell Law Review* 559 (2006), at 587
90. Human Rights Watch & Immigration Equality, Family, Unvalued (2006), at 67-69

91. New York City Gay and Lesbian Anti-Violence Project, New York Lesbian, Gay, Transgender and Bisexual Domestic Violence Report (2005), at 4 and 7

92. National Coalition of Anti-violence Programs, LGBT domestic violence in 2003 (2004), at 23

93. Amnesty International, Stonewalled, Police abuses and misconduct against lesbian, gay, bisexual and transgender people in the U.S. (2005), at 84

94. This is also explained in National Center for Lesbian Rights, Transgender Law Center, Trans Realities (2003) at http://www.nclrights.org/publications/transrealities0803.htm

95. S. Minter, Transgender people and Marriage: the Importance of Legal Planning (2002), at http://www.nclrights.org/publications/tgmarriage.htm

96. National Center for Lesbian Rights, Transgender Law Center, Trans Realities (2003) at http://www.nclrights.org/publications/transrealities0803.htm

97. National Center for Lesbian Rights, Testimonies submitted to the National Prison Rape Elimination Commission on August 15, 2005

98. R. Estrada, J. Marksamer, Lesbian, Gay, Bisexual and Transgender Young People in State Custody: Making the Child Welfare and Juvenile Justice System Safe for all Youth through Litigation, Advocacy and Education, forthcoming on Temple Law Review, Summer 2006

99. Gay, Lesbian and Straight Education Network, From Teasing to Torment: School Climate in America (2005), at 7

100. Gay, Lesbian and Straight Education Network, From Teasing to Torment: School Climate in America (2005), at 7

101. National Gay and Lesbian Task Force, Family Policy – Issues affecting Gay, Lesbian, Bisexual and Transgender Families (2002), at 107

102. National Coalition of Anti-violence Programs, Anti-lesbian, gay, bisexual and transgender violence in 2002 (2003), at 19

103. Lofton v. Secretary of Department of Children and Family Services, F.3d 804 (11th Cir. 2004) , rehearing en banc denied, 377 F.3d 1275 (11th. Cir. 2004), petition for cert. to the U.S.

Supreme Court denied, 125 S. Ct. 869 (2005); see also Nancy Marcus, Beyond Romer and Lawrence: the right to privacy comes out of the closet, 15 Columbia Journal of Gender and Law 355, June 22, 2006

104. Human Rights Campaign, The Cost of Marriage Inequality to Children and their Same-sex Parents (2004), at 9-11

105. www.hrc.org/Template.cfm?Section=Homeownership1& Template=/ ContentManagement/ContentDisplay.cfm & ContentID=18619

7

Promotion and Protection of Rights of Intersex People

Intersex people have the same rights as everyone else under international human rights law. But there do not appear to be any relevant international human rights standards about intersex people. There is little guidance on the application of human rights for intersex people, and this causes difficulties in some areas. In 2004, the Human Rights Commission noted that by difficulties for intersex people were ... the lack of recognition that they exist, and the problems that arise when they are assigned a sex which they would not choose for themselves. International literature shows that debate about the human rights of intersex people is increasing.

Section 15 of the Judicial Matters Amendment Bill, B – 2004, seeks to amend the Promotion of Equality and Prevention of Unfair Discrimination Act, 2000 (PEPUDA), so as to extend the application of the Act expressly to include intersexed persons. There being considerable ignorance about Intersex, most South Africans and many legislators are unlikely to have prior knowledge as to why the it is desirable and necessary to ensure that intersexed persons are explicit beneficiaries of the provisions of PEPUDA. The first and primary purpose of this submission is to explain why this amendment is desirable and necessary. Secondly, there being a definition of "intersexed" in an existing Act, the submission will propose a slight amendment of the definition of "intersex" in order to ensure the compatibility of the definitions.

Intersexed people, to whom the term "hermaphrodites" also

refers, are people whose physical sexual differentiation at birth is not typical. This may be the case at the level of the chromosomal pattern of the person, it may be evident in the internal structures of reproduction, in the makeup of the sex-glands, in the balance of sex-hormones, or in the structure of the external sex-organs. In many but not all cases, the external sex organs are ambiguous. There are only two checkboxes, "male" and "female", in most Western-based legal frameworks, only one of which can be ticked off however ambiguous the sexual anatomy. Although a sex description as male or as female is generally given to intersexed infants at or some time after birth, the experience of intersexed activists shows that the gender assignation is often arbitrary and is at best a judicious guess at the optimal gender of rearing which may be proven wrong in time.

Many distinct syndromes are covered by the umbrella-term "intersexuality" and yield sexual anatomy which is ambiguous or otherwise atypical in some way or other. Some of the major intersex syndromes are as follows:

- One common intersex syndrome is called adrenal hyperplasia, in which over-active adrenal glands produce substances similar to male hormones which cause foetuses which would otherwise have developed along female lines to develop along male lines to a lesser or greater degree instead. The physical appearance of people affected particularly strongly by this syndrome, including that of the sex organs, is masculine and such people tend to experience themselves as more male than female. For the most part, however, this syndrome yields ambiguous genitalia.
- Another major syndrome is called Androgen Insensitivity Syndrome (AIS). In this syndrome, a foetus has a genetic structure which usually results in development along male lines under the influence of male hormones. A gene is passed on, however, which results in the cells of the body being unable to "read" male hormones (androgen) in a way which causes the

body to develop along male lines: the cells of the body are insensitive to androgen to a greater or lesser degree. As a consequence, the body develops along female lines in direct proportion to the degree of the androgen insensitivity. Classification at birth tends to be as female in such cases, and those affected by complete or a relatively high degree of androgen insensitivity invariably experience themselves as female. The more common scenario of partial degrees of the insensitivity to male hormones results in external sexual organs which are ambiguous to a greater or lesser degree, depending on the extent of the insensitivity.

- In Klinefelter Syndrome, the chromosomal pattern is XXY rather than XX pure and simple, which typically (but not invariably) yields a female bodily type and XY pure and simple, which typically (but again, not invariably) yields a male bodily type. Those with this syndrome tend to be classified as male at birth, but are prone to develop bodily types which are ambiguous. The development of large breasts at puberty is fairly common, and gender-identity is often ambiguous.
- There are many more identifiable syndromes. It is important to note, however, that in a significant number of intersexed people the cause of the ambiguous or otherwise atypical sexual anatomy is quite simply not known.

The most important reason for the amendment to PEPUDA, however, is that it will close a major loophole in South African law as it stands which allows almost limitless discrimination in theory, provided that it is on the sole ground of intersexuality.

The terms "sex" and "gender", as used in the Equality Clause of the Bill of Rights and in PEPUDA, is not defined currently and therefore rests upon standard lexical definitions. Standard lexical definitions define the terms dichotomously when applied to human beings, recognising only male and female and incorporating no recognition of intermediate or non-standard sexual differentiation. Intersex is therefore excluded implicitly from the scope of these terms in the lexical sense on which their use in law is based.

There is a piece of case-law, Wood v CG Studios, which brings out the implications of this. The case in question was an American one. A Ms Woods was fired in Pennsylvania when her employers learned that she was intersexed. Ms Woods challenged the dismissal, arguing that her employers had violated a Pennsylvania statute similar to our Equality Clause affording protection against dismissal on grounds of sex or gender, as well as on a number of other grounds. The court found against Ms Woods, arguing that the terms "sex" and "gender" in the statute, resting as they did on lexical definitions, afforded protection against dismissal of a person because that person was a man or because that person was a woman. The logic of the argument of the court was that the statute did not prohibit the dismissal of someone by reason of the fact that the person in question was intersexed. In 1996, a report was prepared by the South African Law Commission in or around 1996 at the request of the Minister of Justice, in which what was to become The Alteration of Sex Description Bill was first considered formally. The report focused primarily on transsexuality, but also touched on intersex. Commenting on the Equality Clause, the authors of the report noted that it afforded no protection either to those who were transsexual or to the intersexed. It is clear that the reasoning of the authors of the report is similar to that of the court in the Wood v CG Studios case.

As matters stand in South Africa, intersex does not fall within the scope of the term "sex" by reason of standard lexical definitions. Intersex is therefore not a listed ground in the context of the Equality Clause and PEPUDA, in which discrimination is deemed to be unfair until proven to be fair. It is an analogical ground at best, in which the burden of proof is reversed. Discrimination is deemed to be fair until and unless proven to be unfair by the party suffering the discrimination. Thus, it is currently incumbent upon anyone intersexed suffering discrimination by sole reason of being intersexed to prove that the discrimination is unfair.

At this stage, another consequence of the lexical definitions needs to be considered. The terms "sex" and "gender", as applied to human beings, form part of a linked lexical group which includes person in the sense of natural person and human being. The dichotomous definition of "sex", in terms of which any human being is either determinately and unequivocally male or determinately and unequivocally female affects the lexical senses of these other terms. This being the case, it is possible to argue that someone whose sex is neither determinately and unequivocally male or determinately and unequivocally female does not satisfy the at least one criterion of what it is to be a natural person of a human being in law. Given the need for locus standi in South African law in order to challenge discrimination formally or to be represented in such a legal challenge against discrimination, a possible form of discrimination on the sole ground of intersexuality is to argue that an intersexed person lacks the locus standi necessary to challenge discrimination. This move is potentially self-vindicating. It discriminates against intersexed people on the sole grounds of their being intersexed. Given that intersex is not one of the listed grounds at present, this form of discrimination is to be deemed fair, the burden of proof that it is unfair resting with the intersexed person or that person's legal representatives. The effect of the discrimination, however, is to render it impossible for the intersexed person or that person's legal representatives to challenge the fairness of that discrimination or indeed of any other form of discrimination provided that it is on the sole ground of intersexuality. A loophole is thus available which makes it theoretically possible to deny any or all rights to a person on the sole ground that the person in question is intersexed. This would clearly be a gross injustice, and the possibility of any such move must be blocked legislatively in the interests of justice.

The proposed amendment to PEPUDA blocks any such move by the statutory stipulation that intersex forms part of the meaning of the term "sex" in PEPUDA and, by interpretation, in the Equality Clause itself. It achieves a great deal simply and elegantly, in a way which engages with the linguistic intuitions of most people. Asked whether non-standard sexual differentiation (that is to say intersexuality) is or is not part of the meaning of the term "sex", anyone possessed of reason will surely say that it is indeed part of the meaning of the term "sex".

Intersex is a challenge for Human rights and Citizenship rights, by Annette Bromdal[1] where she has mentioned that since the South African society, like many other societies, strongly lives by the belief that there are only two sexes and genders, this implies that intersex infants do not fit in and become walking pathologies who must be 'fixed' to become 'normal'. Moreover, since most genital corrective surgeries are imposed without being medically or surgically necessary, and are generally imposed before the age of consent (18), to children concerned, are generally not asked for their opinion regarding the surgery. Lastly because early corrective surgery can have devastating life lasting consequences, this ultimately means that the child's human rights and citizenship rights are of a concern. This conclusion do however not ignore the consequences one has to endure for the price of being 'different'.

Intersex has become the focus of public interest because of the media storm around the questioning of Caster Semenyo's sex. Exemplary post-apartheid constitution of 1996, with its Bill of Rights and Equality Clause, seemed at first glance to afford intersexed South African unassailable legal protection. I would like to share here some of the experience of intersex people. According to them the law has been bolstered since then, but awareness of this fact is needed to afford protection to intersexed people in practice.

Before 2006, when an obscure judicial amendment— comprising two simple definitions — was signed into law, being found to be intersexed opened up all one's rights to challenge. But the promulgation of the Judicial Matters Amendment Act of 2005 changed this technically.

Theoretically, this Act guaranteed protection to the intersexed. Two statutory definitions turned the technical trick. The trouble was that the amendment entered the statute book by stealth: its existence and far-reaching implications have evaded attention until now in a context in which the invisibility of the intersexed, bar a handful of notable exceptions, testifies to an entrenched culture of shame, secrecy and stigmatisation.

The amendment was drafted because an American case made it clear to them that the Equality Clause did not protect the intersexed. An American federal court found that the firing of a woman because she was born intersexed did not breach a Pennsylvania equality statute similar to their Equality Clause.

The statute forbade discrimination on grounds of sex. The court argued that "sex", undefined in the statute, was to be understood in its ordinary dictionary sense. So it referred to the state of being "male and not female" or "female and not male". The upshot: it didn't protect the intersexed.

Our Equality Clause rules discrimination on certain listed grounds, including sex, unfair unless and until proved fair, but "sex" was not defined in statute. The dictionary definition of "sex" — male, female and nothing else — therefore governed its interpretation. "Human being" and "[natural] person" are also defined as having a sex in exclusively binary terms. The intersexed, somewhere in between, could thus be argued to be neither human beings nor natural persons.

The potential consequences were terrifying. Intersex was an "analogical ground" of discrimination rather than a listed ground in the Equality Clause. Unlike discrimination on a listed ground, discrimination on an analogical ground is deemed fair until proven unfair. The burden of proof rests on the victims.

In South African law, one needs locus standi, the right to address the court, to mount a legal challenge. Since the intersexed did not fit workaday definitions of "human beings" and "[natural] persons", arguably they lacked the locus standi to challenge this or any other type of discrimination. It followed that the intersexed, because they were intersexed, had no secure rights — not even to dignity or to life itself.

The obvious remedy was to add "intersex" directly to the Equality Clause's listed grounds. Amendment of the Equality Clause wasn't feasible. The Act begins with a schedule of definitions. Adding two definitions — "'sex' includes intersex" and "'intersex' means a congenital sexual differentiation which is atypical, to whatever degree" — would make intersex part of the meaning of "sex" in the Equality Clause. In January 2006, the definitions became law in the Judicial Matters Amendment Act, 2005. Their technical implications are substantial. Intersexed people had not had an unimpugnable right — even to life — before. Now, by statute, they are bona fide human beings in South African law, protected from discrimination on the grounds that they are intersexed.[2]

According to intersex people stereotypes influenced the discrimination they experienced:

Some of us are still haunted by the spectre of our identity as circus freaks in the not-too-distant past. It is time that our identities and experiences were given the same respect as the rest of the community. (Woman born with an intersex condition)

It's seen as a medical problem to be fixed. (Intergender person)

Intersex people had a range of views about gender, gender identity and biological sex. Some had a gender identity that was neither female nor male.

My gender identity is unequivocally female, and it has been dearly won and maintained. While it seems to fascinate some non-intersex folk that there could be a state of engenderment outside a male–female binary, I find that labelling to be demeaning when applied to me. Although some intersex people might want to avoid rigid gender labelling, I would not like to see a situation where a history of intersexuality was always equated with gender fluidity: I am hurt when my gender is not affirmed in the same way as the general population. The 'neither-one-nor-t'other' jokes are not funny to me. (Woman born with an intersex condition)

Intersex people are entitled to protection from discrimination and have the right to make complaints of sex discrimination under the Human Rights Act 1993. Intersex people said that in most cases a sex (either male or female) had been assigned to them by the time their birth was registered. For some the sex assigned at birth was appropriate. However, others felt very strongly that the sex recorded on their birth certificate was an inaccurate record of their biological sex and conflicted with their gender identity.

Intersex people's concerns about the need for legal documents that reflected their appropriate sex mirrored the concerns of trans people. However, intersex people were concerned they could face additional barriers when attempting to change their records under the Births, Deaths and Marriages Registration Act 1995. In particular, they were unsure how a 'physical conformity' test would be applied to an intersex person, and whether it would require additional surgeries to reverse operations performed when they were children. In some cases it would be extremely difficult or impossible to recreate parts of the body that had been surgically removed. The prospect of additional, often expensive, surgery was daunting for some given the trauma associated with operations performed on them as children.

In one case, the intersex person's birth had first been registered as 'indeterminate', and was subsequently changed to 'female'. According to this person the application for amendment was declined by the Registrar for the following reasons:

While I appreciate your approach, I do not believe it would be appropriate for me to determine your application simply as an error of fact on your birth registration. That is, I would have to be satisfied that the decision to assign the 'female' gender to you was wrong and that you have always, since your birth, been a person of indeterminate sex. From the supporting documentation ... which suggests that you underwent surgery to feminise your genitalia ... I would not think you could support that factual claim, at least from a physical conformation sense. (Letter from Registrar of Births, Death and Marriages'

September 1999)

The Registrar noted at the time that the provisions in the Act 'have never to date been used by a person who is applying to have the gender on their birth registration changed to indeterminate or intersex'. One submitter has recently filed such an application under section 85 of the Act.

The Office of the Privacy Commissioner noted that in 2003 it received a complaint from an individual identified as intersex at birth who underwent surgery as a baby in an attempt to assign a particular gender:

The assigned gender was recorded on the birth certificate and for a number of years this person has been involved in ongoing struggles with various government departments in an attempt to have the birth certificate details corrected to show either an 'indeterminate' gender or the person's current gender status. They reported difficulties in applying for jobs, enrolling at educational institutions, holding a driver's licence and a number of other situations in which personal identification is required. This person described feelings of humiliation, hurt and a loss of dignity as a result.

For intersex people who identify as neither fully male nor female, an (X) passport was the one official document offering an opportunity to have their sex recorded as indeterminate. Some intersex people had difficulties obtaining a (X) or (–) passport because the policies of the Passport Office were designed primarily for trans people, not intersex people. The absence of clear policies resulted in applications by intersex people being delayed:

It took six months to get my sex omitted on my passport because there was nothing in the policy manual about intersex.... In the end one guy got to make the decision himself. He's been brilliant. (Intersex person)

Intersex people have the same rights as all other people to the full protection and promotion of their human rights. There are significant human rights issues affecting intersex people that merit urgent consideration so as to improve their dignity, equality and security. The number of live births recorded as indeterminate is not an accurate basis for estimating the size of the intersex population because most intersex children appear to be assigned a sex at birth (or soon after) and have their birth registered as male or female rather than indeterminate. Other intersex conditions will not become evident until a young person reaches puberty, and has already spent many years living as male or female. For these reasons very few people born with intersex conditions are registered as having an indeterminate sex. There are a number of parallels between the experiences of many intersex and trans people. Both groups asserted the right to be themselves without fear of discrimination and to be treated with dignity and respect when they seek medical support. While most intersex and trans-people are likely to identity as male or female, a third option is important to some intersex, androgynous or 'third sex' people. This includes the ability to obtain an (X) passport.

However, there are some very significant issues that are specific to intersex people, particularly in relation to medical procedures performed on children and young people with intersex conditions. Having access to full medical records, including those used as the basis for any legal change of sex, is critically important for intersex people. The absence of such records compounds the invisibility, secrecy and shame felt by many.

The above experience was shared by only one intersex community group contracted by Intersex Awareness New Zealand established as the Intersex Trust Aotearoa New Zealand. The trust has a website with information.

On May 27, the Human Rights Commission of the city and country of San Francisco held the world's first official hearing on the human rights violation of people born with intersex conditions. Among speakers were intersex activities Thea Hilman, Betsy Driver, Hida Viloria, Blue, David Cameron, Peter Trinkle, and Suegec Tamar – Mattis, who shared their personal experiences. Other supporters, including parents of intersex individuals, scholars and medical professionals also gave testimonies demanding measures to preserve intersex human rights.

In the year 2009 The Australian Human Rights Commission has lodged its submission to the National Human Rights Consultation, formalising its key recommendation that the Australian Parliament should enact a national Human Rights Act.

Commission President, Catherine Branson QC said, "Australia needs a system of government which makes sure that all people, no matter who they are, what they do, or where they live, have a safety net to protect their fundamental human rights, and a Human Rights Act would assist achievement of this aim".

President Branson said a Human Rights Act would work to prevent human rights problems before they occur because:

- Parliament would be asked to consider human rights when making new laws;
- the Australian Government would be required to respect human rights when developing policy, making decisions and delivering services;
- federal courts and tribunals would have to take human rights into account when interpreting laws;
- if a federal court found that a law was inconsistent with human rights, Parliament would be notified and required to respond; and
- individuals whose human rights were breached would be able to seek remedies.

In over two decades of experience consulting with people in Australia about their human rights concerns, Human Rights Commissioner, Graeme Innes said the Commission has clearly heard that people care about their fundamental human rights and think that there should be better protection of these rights.

"Human rights should be considered every time a government law, policy or other decision is made," Commissioner Innes said. "A Human Rights Act would not only help promote the development of a culture of respect for human rights in Australia, it would also introduce greater transparency and accountability into our system of government."

President Branson said a national Human Rights Act would be an extremely positive development for Australia. "Not only would a Human Rights Act assist people in Australia to become aware of the human rights that the Australian Government has pledged to protect, but it would assist in awareness and understanding of their own responsibility to respect the rights of others."

President Branson said a stronger human rights culture would further build respect for the human dignity, freedom and equality of all people in Australia.

Intersex Round Table convened by Human Rights Commission in Auckland on February 2010 been conducted and it was attended by 20 people including five intersex people, two people representing families of children with intersex medical condition, six health professionals from five disciplines (counselling, midwifery, paediatrics, endocrinology, sexual health and neonatal nursing), two academics and a government agency. Both New Zealand organization providing information and education around intersex issues (IANZ and CAHNZ) were represented.[3]They focus on the support for intersex people and their parents.

There has been a world-wide grassroots movement of support groups, particularly on the internet. However it can be difficult to publicise groups and their availability for referrals, particularly if health professionals do not facilitate access to such information.

It was acknowledged that when a baby is born with an intersex medical condition there is often a huge grieving process for parents. Having a child with an intersex condition may raise specific issues for a parent, so support from other extended family members is very valuable.

The various stages of grief may include shock, numbness, confusion, denial and anger. It can be particularly hard for parents to deal with uncertainty, when decisions are being delayed in the best interests of the child. Sometimes this means a parent literally cannot hear what a health professional is telling them "All I could see was his mouth opening and closing". Parents need:

- a physician with good information or who is able to make a referral to someone else who is more informed;
- information and resources as a bridge over this space of numbness, confusion and shock, and time to sift through it;
- a resource that provides answers to the typical questions asked by family members, schools, etc.

Components of Education

a) the clinical information about various conditions and

b) the framework within which that information is provided.

The context in which intersex issues are discussed is important including whether it builds understanding about diversity of bodies and sexes. Parents often have concerns about how their intersex adolescent's sense of themself sexually might be affected if they have a body that is not definitively male or female. Being able to talk about diversity of sexes, gender identities and sexual orientation may help reduce the stigma associated with having an intersex medical condition.

There is a significant group of people with negative past experiences. What support do Intersex need? Is it important to acknowledge past mistakes, for example through some type of formal apology, as has been proposed in North America?

For some intersex adults there are significant unanswered questions including around:

- the nature of their medical condition and whether it was classified as an intersex condition (e.g. some forms of Hypospadia were deemed to be cosmetic surgery).

- the extent of medical or surgical interventions performed when they were young (particularly when medical records are not available).
- whether hormones such as Stilbestrol can be historically linked to the incidence of intersex medical conditions.

Typically follow-up has been appalling and yet it is essential in order to know long term outcomes. Follow-up is hampered by funding structures which require patients to move from adolescent services to adult services. Some conditions only emerge later in life and/or young people may not feel able to speak up about their personal wishes whilst still dependent on their parents. More qualitative data is needed which asks intersex adults to describe the long term outcomes of having, or not having, medical and surgical intervention. Access to the Special High Cost treatment pool funding for corrective surgeries is only available via a DHB specialist. This can be a barrier for an intersex person if they do not have support from medical professionals.

Education for Health Professionals

Given relatively low numbers, paediatricians and physicians may not have any prior experience, and treatment can be based on personal views and/or biases. Medical practice remains highly variable. There is a need for:

- national resources and ways to share them more easily, including through websites
- resources available to the current health workforce that then get incorporated into the teaching curriculum for new nurses, social workers and other health professionals
- knowledge about specific health issues and medical care required for intersex people as they age (for example health issues due to long term use of hormones and/or arising from having a body that is different)
- a stronger focus on psychological issues particularly for those who do not fit easily within binary sex categories of male or female.

- clarity about differences between the health issues for trans-people and those related to intersex medical conditions. While there can be overlap for some people, the distinctions are very important.

Even for an informed health professional, these are still incredibly hard conversations to have with new parents. Early reactions from parents and health professionals are very important.

How can parents and health professionals be supported so they are able to react in ways that are affirming for children born with diverse bodies and/or with intersex medical conditions? Suggestions included:

- providing midwives with opportunities to do role plays about those important 'first words'.
- learning from advocates' personal experiences either directly or through documentaries about and interviews with intersex people.
- drawing from what happens at the Royal Children's Hospital in Melbourne, where specialists and advocates work together to give families information needed to identify possible options.

Legal Recognition

- having sex details listed as X or indeterminate is currently seen as a temporary status (e.g. on passport), used by trans people early on in their transition. However for some intersex and/or trans people it is their preferred long term sex.
- it is hard to access clear information about the options for intersex people wanting to change sex details (and how these differ for those under the age of 18 compared to adults) or to correct details on a birth registration.
- more flexibility is needed in the legal recognition process so that families do not have to go back to the Family Court multiple times as a child's sex / gender identity becomes clearer

- in a recent Family Court case an intersex person was able to have their birth certificate corrected to indeterminate. What are the legal implications for sex-specific legislation including the right to marry?
- there is value in educating Family Court staff about issues for intersex people
- for some intersex people, having a third 'other' or 'indeterminate' option on other forms is the preferred option too.
- When might it be useful for intersex people to have the option of identifying themselves on such forms? How could that information be collected in a way that protects people's privacy and potentially identifies health and other needs for this population group?

Informed consent

- Capacity to consent changes over time. There is a notion of ongoing consent especially as someone obtains more information and/or is better able to understand information they receive.
- Another distinction can be made between informed consent and the term 'informed choice' which requires sufficient information and time for someone to consider a range of alternatives.
- The assumption can be that parents have full information, whereas that is not always the case.
- Issues of informed consent / choice place a huge burden on parents who are trying to make the best decision for their child. Parents have to live with their choice.
- When a parent is traumatised and unsupported, how does that impact on their ability to give informed consent?
- If surgery is performed in Melbourne, does that fall under New Zealand or Australian law? Some units in Australia won't do any surgery if the patient is less than

15 years old, whereas others such as the Royal Children's Hospital in Melbourne may do surgery if someone has Congenital Adrenal Hyperplasia (CAH).

Parents' rights and children's rights

The questions raised in this discussion suggest there would be value in having further dialogue about the rights of the child, particularly those instances where this is potential conflict between the child's and the parent/s' rights

- A parent is the key focus at a birth and is the child's world - however parental consent is not the sole consideration.
- Who focuses on the specific rights of the child - particularly in instances where there may be conflict with the needs or views of the parent/s? One example might be parents not wanting a medical practitioner to disclose information to their intersex child.
- When can a third party usefully clarify these issues?
- Is there a role for intersex advocates in presenting the full range of options e.g. that while most children and young people with CAH will choose to be raised as female, there may be a minority who do not want any feminising surgery.
- Is it ever appropriate to not give parents the option of surgery? Or do parents always have a role in making this decision as part of their parental responsibility?
- How do parents respond if they are encouraged to delay surgery or are told that surgery is not an option?
- It is unlawful to discriminate against intersex people in areas of public life including when they are accessing health services.
- Sections 204A and B of the Crimes Act 1961 criminalise female genital mutilation. Could it also criminalise some forms of genital surgery?

- Section 204A does not apply to a medical or surgical procedure that is performed by a medical practitioner for the benefit of that person's physical or mental health.
- Section 204A states that cultural or religious beliefs or other custom or practice about "what is necessary or desirable" shall not be taken into account when determining if such a procedure should be performed.
- Prior to 1996 when these sections were added, the only issue was whether or not a patient had consented to the procedures.

Roundtable participants contributed the following suggestions and examples of current better practice after a baby is born with a possible intersex medical condition. People considered it necessary to continue developing better practice that is flexible enough to encompass diverse needs and intersex adults' knowledge of longer term outcomes, Initial support

- acknowledge and provide support to families.
- the support needed is not just medical but also counselling and psychological support, including from someone else who has been through the experience themselves (another parent, an adult with a similar medical condition).
- allow time to get a diagnosis.
- do not medically classify a child if there is any doubt about the sex that the child should be reared as. For some intersex medical conditions it is very difficult to predict how children will wish to be raised. Even for other conditions, there are likely to be a range of different decisions.
- in the interim, given we live in a binary world, parents often assign a name for practical purposes, including the birth notice and a sex / gender to use when necessary

Providing Information to a Child

"Being told by my parents what had happened would have totally changed things."

- support parents so that hopefully they will talk about the medical condition naturally from an early age i.e. help the child know and accept they are different
- generally parents will take a health professional's advice about disclosure but it can be more complex if there are multiple health professionals
- preferably there is no lower age limit for talking with a child, so that information can be added sequentially at a level and time that a child can cope
- increase the complexity of information as a child becomes a teenager
- from intersex peoples' experiences, broader conversations outside the family are important, especially if the family dynamic discourages talking about bodies or sex, or if the child is taught to hide their body
- the Royal Children's Hospital in Melbourne collates comprehensive medical files that can be available to an intersex person later in life. This is self-empowering and very helpful if corrective surgery is wanted at a later date. It also helps to fill in gaps as it is very hard for parents to remember ever detail over time.

Avoid/Delay all but Life-saving Surgery

- generally avoid any surgical interventions until the child is old enough to give informed consent e.g. don't remove gonads (whereas this used to be standard practice)
- the exceptions are where surgical intervention is necessary to preserve a life e.g. if an obstruction is causing kidney damage.

Initial discussions in this roundtable discussion identified a range of perspectives on when surgery might be medically necessary and whether newer surgical techniques still reduce sensation (especially in the absence of longer term follow-up studies once a person is sexually active).

Establishing a Response Network

Many roundtable participants were interested in working together to coordinate care available and to ensure more consistent adoption of better practice. It was envisaged this would involve a multi-disciplinary team including intersex advocates that could receive referrals and provide follow-up support to families. This would include directing people to advocacy groups.

Some initial discussion points were:

- The value of learning from the experience of multi-disciplinary teams overseas. These often operate from a central location or centre of excellence. However a 'network of excellence' is likely to be more feasible in New Zealand, linking people from around the country. The increasing availability of health records in electronic format makes coordinating care easier across distances.
- What would be the scope of such a group? There are always likely to be definitional issues about which medical conditions are defined as 'intersex'. Greater understanding about the diversity of intersex conditions (and people's differing experiences of the same condition) would ideally mean referrals were widely available for any child or adult requiring support.
- Such a network would require some funding from the Ministry of Health to set it up and then need to be promoted to health professionals in order to receive referrals. Centralised bulk funding sources may be an option, with referrals from those DHBs that don't have experience in this field.
- A contact list was circulated and one of the clinicians offered to be the first point of contact, without assuming that the process will be medically led. The next step would probably be an initial teleconference. The Commission's video-conference facilities in its Auckland, Wellington and Christchurch offices could possibly be available, and also allow up to five further sites to be linked in by phone.

The Commission is updating its 2004 report on the status of human rights in New Zealand. *Human Rights in NZ Today 2010* will include a chapter looking at the separate but related human rights issues around diverse sexes, sexual orientations and gender identities. It will be an opportunity to highlight the most pressing human rights issues for intersex people. The Asia Pacific OutGames in Wellington in March 2011 will include a human rights conference. There is the option of proposing presentations, panels or workshops on intersex human rights issues.

Many people uncomfortable with the term intersex, new terminology emerged from the US based consortium on Disorders of Sexual Development.[4] The new DSD terminology is seen as stigmatising by many intersex people but has significant traction in medical communities (partly because it is used for diagnoses and developing treatment pathways). Intersex people are increasingly standing up for their rights and advocating for a climate that does not stigmatise diversity of bodies and/or identities. A number of roundtable participants advocated strongly that while some surgeries are medically necessary, any other surgeries should be left until a child is old enough to make their own decision and give informed consent.

Discrimination on the basis of sex is a violation of human right. People do not need surgery just because their genitals are ambiguous. Many intersex people have an "intersex identity" and their anatomy feels appropriate to them. Intersex person gladly identity themselves as "intersex" if the culture permitted. Intersexuality is natural. Intersex people should come out of the closet. There should be no secrecy or shame. Intersex is god Gift, it is beautiful, they are the complete human being. Intersex people do not need to change; the culture needs to change. Society needs to be enlightened, and the culture should change to acknowledge and accommodate intersex people. Media portrayals reinforce gender stereotypes and do not allow room for diversity. When media portrays what is feminine or masculine, where do intersex people fit in?

NOTES & REFERENCES

1. http://oiiaustralia.com/8276/intersex_challange_ human_rights_citizenship+rights_annette_brmdal
2. www.intersex.org.za
3. http://www.hrc.co.nz/home/hrc/humanrightsenvironment/actionontheirnasgendering/intersexpeople
4. http://www.dsdguidelines.org.

8

Conclusion

In the last twenty years, much progress has been made in terms of improving the medical and social attitude towards people with intersex, but that significant work remains to be done to ensure that children born with sex anomalies will be treated in a way that privileges their long-term well-being over societal norms. While feminist scholars have been critically important in developing the theoretical underpinnings of the intersex rights movement and sometime in carrying out the day to day political work of that movement, there have been intellectual and political problems with some feminist approaches to intersex. Biology does matter in determining one's sexual orientation, but at the same time, culture plays a central role as well. Culture and biology interact with one another.

Historically, intersex had been a much broader and inclusive category, and included many people who would now be considered transsexual, as well as many homosexuals. This was an idea that can be traced back to Magnus Hirschfeld, and up until the 1960's was still current – anybody not part of the binary-sexed heterosexual normality was in some way intersex. There ware assumed to be reasons for this that were grounded in biology. With John Money, the emancipation of gay and lesbian people, and surgery for transsexuals, the focus on biological causes became restricted; being gay or lesbian was no longer seen as a sickness, gender identity was developed to explain the sense of sex one identified as , and gender behaviour was seen as rooted in social development. Transsexuals were increasingly identified as biological men or women with gender identity in conflict with their physiology. This left only those with issues that had clear biological markers as being subject to biological causes.

The assignment of the term intersex has tended to be applied to people assigned and reinforced as female, while those assigned male have been discounted. This has tended to be because those assigned male have been seen as less severely affected by their manifestations of these issues than those assigned female. The way this has worked has been that intersex has been thought of predominantly affecting people assigned female, rather than male and thus a problem for women and feminists.

I believe that 'Intersex' is simply a part of human variation. It is not a 'disorder' but a 'natural order'. The treatment is not for intersex people but for the system of the society. Vast majority of people born with intersex conditions live normally as a woman or man, and do not view themselves as member of a different gender/sex category. Most people born with intersex condition do not think "intersex" to be who they are; it is simply a medical condition or a lived history of medicalization. Most people with intersex conditions would answer "no" if they are asked "are you intersex?" Most people who would check "intersex" are probably not intersex, but non-intersex individuals who do not know what intersex is. These are the people who feel that they do not belong to "norms" of being either male or female who mistakenly think "intersex" describes who they are. This is a very common misperception among some people. To list "intersex" along with "male" and "female" gives the false impression that one cannot be male or female if she or he has intersex condition. This hurts people with intersex conditions and for this the 'social norms' is fully responsible.

Many terms have been used to describe people of diverse sex and/or gender identities. Some of these include a gender, androgynous, cross dresser, drugqueen, gender fluid, genderqueen, intergender, intersex, neutrots, pansexual,pan gendered, third gender, third sex, transgender, transexed, transsexual, hijra, kinnar etc. and without sexed gender identity. In addition, there are culturally specific terms, such as sistergirl and brotherboy, which are used by some Aboriginal and Torres Strait Islander people. But whatever terms have been used to describe intersex people doesn't matter for them but what matters for them is the legal identity, social identity and their identity as a natural human being with all the natural rights including the right to live happily in the society with other human being.

Intersex is neither a medical nor a social pathology. Intersex genitals are not a medicl problem. They may signal and underlying metabolic concern, but they themselves are not diseased. They just look different. The autonomy and right to self-determination of the person with an intersex condition is violated by surgery-centered model. In the concealment model, surgeries are done without truly obtaining consent; parents are often not told the failure rate of, lack of evidentiary support for and alternative to surgery. Social distress is a reason to change society, not the body of children. There should be social acceptance of human diversity and also an end to the idea that "difference equals disease". There should be a strong recommendation to avoid harmful or unnecessary genital surgery on infant and children. No surgery should be performed unless it is absolutely necessary for the physical health and comfort of the intersexed child. Any surgery that does not meet these criteria to be essentially elective cosmetic surgery which should be deferred until intersexual child is able to understand the risk and benefits of the proposed surgery and is able to provide appropriate informed consent. "Ambiguous" genitalia do not constitute a disease. They simply constitute a failure to fit a particular (and, at present, a particular demanding) definition of normality. Person with an intersex condition has the right to self-determination where her or his body is concerned. Doing "normalizing" surgeries early without the individual's consent interferes with that right.

Intersex is a community and social concern requiring understanding and support. Counseling should begin as soon as the possibility of intersex arises and as soon as the family needs it. Professional counselors are trained in sex and gender issues, family dynamics, and unexpected birth outcomes should be present. Families should also be actively connected with peer support. They strongly need the support from their social group.

Discrimination is socially constructed and is based on social rules or norms. One may ask what are rules. Simply put, social norms or rules are "ways of doing things" or pattern that become routine over a period of time. The denial of equal status for intersex is based on biological difference as well as notion of equivalent rights. So there is a need to sideline the norms of the society, there is a need to change the patterns of the society and there is a strong need to give equal status to intersex people in the society. There is a need for social awareness programmes. There is a need of laws to reflect the reality of their bodies so that an intersex person can have access to marriage, superannuation, insurance and all the things available only to male and female sex. Intersex people want equal rights without having to pretend their bodies are really male or female. Many people with intersex conditions identify solidly as a man or as a woman, like many non-intersex people. There are some who identif· as a member of an alternative gender, like some non-intersex people. While we support everyone's right to define her or his own identities, we do not believe that people with intersex conditions should be expected to be gender transgressive just because of 'socially not fit' condition.

Medicine cannot determine baby's "true sex". For example, chromosomes do not necessarily dictate one's gender identity, as it is obvious from the fact that most people born with androgen insensitivity syndromes live as women despite their XY chromosomes. In other words: science can measure how large a clitoris is, but cannot conclude how large or small it needs to be. That is a social determination, surgery is just part of a larger pattern of how intersex children are treated; it is also important to stop shame, secrecy and isolation that are socially and medically imposed on children born with intersex conditions under the theory that the child is better off it didn't hear anything about it. Therefore, it's not enough to simply stop the surgery; we need to replace it with social and psychological support as well as open and honest communication. Pronouns should not be based on the shape of one genitalia, but on what the person prefers to be called. For children too young to communicate what his/her preference is, go with the gender assignment parents and doctor agreed on based on their best prediction.

On October 26, 1996, intersex activists from Intersex Society of North America (carrying the sign "Hermaphrodites with Attitude") and other allies from Transsexuals Menace held the first public intersex demonstration in Boston, where American Academy of Pediatrics was holding its annual conference. The action generated a lot of press coverage, and made it difficult for the medical community to continue to neglect their growing movement. That said, events related to Intersex Awareness Day. Intersex was discussed on British TV for the first time in 1996, and became a topic of interest for broadcast TV and radio in the United states and other countries from 1989. Jeffrey Eugendes' novel 'MiddleSex' (2002) is narrated by an intersex character who discuss the societal experience of an intersex person.[1] The Japanese manga series I.S., first published in 2003, features intersex character and how they deal with intersex-related issues and influence the lives of people around them. The multi volume Vorkosigan Saga Science fiction series by Lois McMaster Bujold features the hermaphrodite (Bujold's usage) character Captain Bel Thorne from the socially liberal Beta colony, where hermaphrodites (originally genetically engineered) from a (locally) respected minority of the population.

Intersexuality primarily is an issue of stigma and emotional trauma. In our culture, sexual variation which bless the line between male and female is stigmatized. Intersexuality is so highly stigmatized that, until recently, the phenomenon was little known outside related medical specialties. Thus, the birth of an intersex child is emotionally traumatizing: Parents are traumatized because the birth of a child with sexual ambiguity violates a deeply held world-view, and because it elicits parental feeling of shame and guilt. Intersex child are traumatized because they are made to feel utterly unique, alone, and unacceptable. Intersex individuals are still raised as either male or female in most societies, and this seems unlikely to change. However, these individuals are challenging medical thinking that they should be surgically or hormonally assigned to one sexual category or the other, particularly during infancy or childhood before they have consolidated their gender identity (Intersex Society of North America). In most societies, intersex individual do end up living in one gender role or the other and have either a male or female gender identity. In a few societies there is a distinct social sex role for some intersex individuals and that role is result of their unacceptance from the society. Two examples of this are the turnim man in New Guinea and the Guevodoces in the Dominican Republic. Newborns with these syndromes congenital Adrenal Hyperplasia) may look like girls or boys at birth. However, in some cases the midwives recognize them as intersex, and they are raised in an intersex role. These children masculinize at puberty. According to Society, they are not as females and often assume a male role after puberty. The hijra caste in India includes intersex individuals who may be placed there for raising from childhood, although as I have discussed hijras are predominantly composed of non-intersex males. Medical intervention has been predicted on the notion that quality of life is possible only for individual who conforms to male or female sex and gender. But in recent year, the possibility of a third gender, of non-conformance, has come to the fore. There are several threads to this discourse. Anthropologists and ethnographers have identified third gender categories in many cultures as I have mentioned such as Berdache in Native America, the Hijra in India, the Xanith in Oman, and many other. Non-conforming gender roles are also in evidence in the growing transgender movement, which has rebelled against medical policy which offered services to transsexual only if they conformed adequately to mainstream heterosexual male of female roles. Intersex advocacy movement, represent most forcefully by ISNA, is beginning to speak out against the harms of genital surgery and of secrecy and taboo surrounding intersexuality.

According to ISNA, many intersex people are perfectly comfortable adopting either a male or female gender identity and are not seeking a genderless society or to label themselves as a member of a third gender class. Although it's true that the urge to perform surgeries on intersex children's sex anatomies is sometimes born out of the belief that children must have sex anatomies that are clearly male or female in order to be comfortable in either a male or female gender (and this is clearly a harmful belief born out of antiquated notions about gender identity corresponding directly to genital anatomy), the idea of raising a child as a boy or girl isn't what most adults with intersex conditions point to as their main problem.

In fact, many of the people with intersex we know—both those subjected to early surgeries and those who escaped surgery—very happily accepted a gender assignment of male or female (either the one given them at birth or one they chose later for themselves later in life). Instead, adults with intersex conditions who underwent genital surgeries at early ages most often cite those early genital surgeries and the lies and shame surrounding those procedures as their source of pain. Later in life, like many people with typical anatomies, intersex people take pleasure in what some gender scholars (like Judith Butler) might call doing their gender. Thus, intersex people don't tell us that the very concept of gender is oppressive to them. Instead, it's the childhood surgeries performed on them and the accompanying lies and shame that are problematic.

Again, many of these surgeries are performed with the belief that these procedures will help a child settle into a gendered world, but that doesn't mean the whole system of gender must fall in order for people with intersex conditions to live happy, fulfilling lives. It simply means that these surgeries and the shame that surrounds them are an unfortunate instantiation of problematic gender norms and we should work on ending unwanted surgeries and stigma.

There are, of course, some people with intersex conditions who identify as a third gender or gender queer—just as there are some people with completely typical sex anatomies who don't identify as strictly male or female. The aim of ISNA isn't to undermine these people's goals, or to suggest that people who identify as a third gender don't exist or don't matter, or to suggest that everyone must adopt a gender. Rather, they hope to end painful and unnecessary childhood surgeries that rob people of corporeal autonomy and sexual function because everyone—regardless of gender identity—deserves that. And they hope to end the shame and secrecy that cause so much pain for so many people with intersex conditions.

They hope that scholars, particularly those invested in helping members of marginalized groups gain a voice in conversations about themselves, will take seriously the concerns about surgery, secrecy, and shame raised by intersex people and understand that ISNA and the majority of its constituency don't necessarily share the goal of eradicating the very notion of gender.

Psychologist John Money provided theoretical support for the Hopkins model, arguing that gender identity was largely mutable early in life, that nurture was more important than nature. His chief support for this claim came from a famous case known as "John/Joan." The person at the center, David Reimer, was born an identical twin (not intersex) boy in 1965. While performing a circumcision, a doctor accidentally burned off eight-month-old David's penis. David's parents consulted with the team at Hopkins, and Money recommended they change the sex and gender of their child and raise David as a girl. For decades Money erroneously touted a successful outcome because the child reportedly had become a normal, female-identified, heterosexual girl. The truth was that David had never felt fully female. Indeed, when his parents told him the truth about what happened to him, he immediately re-assumed the gender role of a man.

It is unknown why Money—who in 1953 had found a relatively low rate of psychopathology among adults with intersex—thought people with intersex needed to have their sexes and genders surgically and socially engineered to be psychologically healthy. It is better understood why people did not question Money's controversial theory of nurture-over-nature approach. Surgeons and psychologists liked the theory because it signified that they were providing necessary, good care to "abnormal" children. Feminists liked the theory because they preferred the idea that gender - and therefore gender norms - were socially constructed and malleable. Parents probably liked it because they could be reassured that their queer-bodied children would grow up to be straight-acting adults.

But some people didn't like this system: people who—like David Reimer—felt mistreated at best, and medically assaulted at worst, by their medical treatment. Nevertheless, most stayed silent, believing they were alone in their experiences.

That changed in 1993, when feminist biologist Anne Fausto-Sterling published articles in *The Sciences* and *The New York Times* exposing the basic fact that intersex exists. In response, Cheryl Chase wrote a letter to *The Sciences* announcing the founding of the Intersex Society of North America (ISNA). She founded the group because of her own attempts to recover her history of sex-reassignment in infancy and medically-induced shame, and because of the disinterest of most of her former care providers in what had happened to her. Soon Chase had brought together dozens of people with intersex.

Though ISNA began as a support group, it quickly turned into an advocacy group because its members realized that they had suffered from similar problems. Like many of the early ISNA members, Chase drew on her political consciousness as a lesbian woman to recognize the degree to which intersex had been unnecessarily socially and medically pathologized. With the successes of the women's health movement and the queer rights movements as a backdrop, people with intersex began agitating for openness and reform.

Early on, very few medical professionals recognized ISNA's critiques as legitimate. Many responded that the standard of care was necessary, successful, and justified, even going so far as to actively defend lying to patients about their medical histories. Those at the top simply tried to ignore ISNA. As the leader of the newly formed intersex rights movement, Chase moved rapidly, sometimes able to engage in dialog, and having group protests when doctors would not listen. With her professional background in computer science, she was particularly adept at using the tools of the Internet to spread ISNA's message. ISNA also supported the inquiries of researchers like Suzanne Kessler, Anne Fausto-Sterling, and Alice Dreger, and the organization engaged in media outreach as much as possible.

By about 2001, it had become clear to all that the intersex rights movement was not going away. The claims of activists were illustrated in story after story of problematic intersex treatment, as well as in research that strongly suggested gender identity is not simply a matter of nurture. The fact that medical professionals were unable to produce an intersex patient satisfied with his/her childhood treatment negated the claims that the advocacy groups solely represented the experiences of a disgruntled minority.

I believe that many intersex people have an "Intersex Identity" and their anatomy feels appropriate to them. There are intersex people who gladly identify as "intersex" if the society permitted.

ISNA recommend avoidance of harmful or unnecessary genital surgery on infants and children. No surgery should be performed unless it is absolutely necessary for the physical health and comfort of the intersexual child. They believe any surgery that does not meet these criteria to be essentially elective cosmetic surgery which should be deferred until the intersexual child is able to understand the risks and benefits of the proposed surgery and is able to provide appropriately informed consent. Examples of such cosmetic surgery to be avoided are plastic repair of first degree epispadias or hypospadias (minor displacement of urethral meatus),vaginoplasty, clitoral reduction or recession, and clitorectomy. Examples of conditions which would appear to justify early surgery are severe second or third degree hypospadias (with extensive exposed mucosal tissue vulnerable to infection), chordee (extensive enough to cause pain), bladder exstrophy,and imperforate anus.

The current model insists that healthy emotional development is impossible for a male child with a penis that is "too small," and demands female assignment, with extensive genital surgery. A similar argument is advanced for performing genital surgery on a female child whose clitoris is "too large." These judgments with respect to phallus size are highly subjective and currently, only anecdotal case reports, in which patients are typically "lost to followup," exist to support the case for early intervention.

They believe that for children whose only intersexual anomaly is micropenis or clitoromegaly, and who are physiologically capable of normal puberty, early surgical intervention significantly increases the risk of impaired sexual function later in life. In their experience, some prepubertal children with penile agenesis, micropenis or clitoromegaly may elect, with appropriate support from a qualified psychotherapist, to change sex role and choose medical intervention to facilitate a sex- and gender role congruent puberty.

Counseling for the entire family of a newborn intersexual, and for the intersexual child as soon as s/he is old enough. This should include thorough exploration of all the medical and surgical options open to the intersexual and his/her family and should address the family's feelings about same-sex arousal patterns and behavior since a large minority of intersexuals develop into gay, lesbian, or bisexual adults or choose to change sex—regardless of whether or not early surgical repair or reassignment was performed. This counseling should be performed by a mental health professional with extensive training and experience in psychotherapy and specialized competence in sex therapy and sexological theory. Psychotherapeutic skills are developed through long years of training and the practice of psychotherapy is a full-time profession. While surgeons and endocrinologists have also undergone arduous and extensive training to acquire their specialized medical skills, they typically have little or no mental health training and their busy practices generally do not permit them to obtain the necessary counseling skills. Nonpsychiatrically trained physicians should no more practice psychotherapy than psychiatrists or non-medically trained psychotherapists should perform surgery or prescribe hormones.

The current model dates back to the '50s. In those days, clinicians could safely write patient records, not to mention medical textbook and journal articles, without fear that their patients would ever read what they had written. Today, the ethics of disclosure and autonomy have changed, as has access to medical literature. Many of them have read through all of their medical records and much of the medical literature on intersex. Very few intersexuals remain unaware of their status, but many are prevented, by shame and stigma, from discussing it with anyone. Shame surrounds not only intersexual status, but also damaged erotic function due to genital surgery. It is imperative that intersexuals learn of their status in a properly supportive emotional environment and have access to a peer support group. Many of them, contacting others through the Intersex Society has been a life-changing, or even life-saving, experience. ISNA provides a safe space for them to develop and express healthy identities as intersexuals.

The option of surgical and hormonal intervention should be offered around puberty. Intervention should be undertaken only at the request and with the full informed consent of the intersexual child, including the opportunity to discuss sexual function with adults who have undergone similar surgeries, and validation of the child's right to delay or to choose no surgery at all. Plastic surgery of the genitals is profoundly damaging to erotic function, and the individual choosing surgery must be allowed to evaluate the tradeoff for her/himself.

Finally, many medical professionals began to respond to calls for outcome data, research, full disclosure of information, and revision of homophobic and sexist protocols. The intersex rights movement undoubtedly was helped in its success by surrounding trends in favor of LBGT (lesbian, bi, gay, transgender) rights, patients' rights, and children's rights.

Since 1993, due to increased public education, tens of

millions of people have learned about intersex. Thanks to the internet, thousands of people with intersex have met others like them, in spite of having been told by their doctors they would never be able to do that—their conditions were supposedly so rare.

ISNA members have gone from picket lines to having a seat at the table in medical conferences. They give grand rounds presentations, help with medical school curricular development, and receive emails from physicians asking for our advice on how to handle intersex cases. Their website is recognized as the definitive source for all things intersex, and for being a life-saving porthold for thousands of people desperate for answers and directions to "their tribe". They have convinced hospitals around the world to examine their practices, to find out what has happened to former patients, and to be accountable for the sometimes-poor effects of good intentions.

Over a decade into the work of ISNA, medical professionals are less inclined to lie to patients and parents in intersex cases, are less likely to make openly homophobic or sexist remarks, and are more likely to admit uncertainty about the right course of action. A number of teams are engaged in active outcomes research, though opinions still differ about what outcomes should be sought; some think stable gender identity and heterosexuality are the objective; others suggest it should be lack of depression.) What type of care an individual or family will receive now varies dramatically; what happens to a child with intersex today appears to depend not only on where she or he is born, but who happens to be on call when she or he is born.

But, even today, the goal of many leading teams treating intersex is still to make intersex disappear. Pediatric endocrinologist Maria New, recommends Dexamethasone to women who may be carrying an XX child with CAH; these treatments do not alleviate CAH, it only makes the child's clitoris appear smaller (and, clinicians hope, makes the child less likely to grow up lesbian). Abortion is routinely offered to women who are likely pregnant with children with intersex conditions, including Klinefelter's Syndrome. Many surgeons maintain the paternalistic attitude that they should remove healthy testes from babies with AIS to "spare them the trauma later," thereby denying these girls the opportunity to have a natural puberty and to come to know themselves, in a sexual way, free from surgical scars. Many endocrinologists press unnecessary—sometimes devestating—"normalizing" hormone treatments on patients who are otherwise healthy. Finally, doctors continue constructing vaginas in infants and young children, despite arguments by many medical professionals that early vaginoplasties fail too often and are unnecessary to begin with.

By contrast, as in the women's rights movement, the civil rights movement, and the LGBT rights movements, the goal of intersex advocacy groups is to have people understand intersex conditions as human rights issues. ISNA maintains as its fundamental principle the principle also fundamental to the women's health movement and the LBGT rights movements: that one's genitals are primarily for one's own use, not for the comfort of others.

Treat any problems the patient present and wants treated but do not consider the intersex condition itself as a disorder, consider it as a natural variation, one of the many differences to be expected in any normal population. The stigma of the label "disorder" should be replaced by "natural order", "difference" or "variation". Intersexuality is natural. Intersex people should come out of the closet. There should be no secrecy or shame. Intersex people do not need to change; the society need to change. "Right to life" is not only for male and female but also for the people who are naturally different from male and female. They equally deserve their position as a human being in the society. We should not forget that they are not the people with disease but they are people like us with little biological difference. They have the same heart and soul like us. If the society give them recognition as human being there is no need for them to become hijra, kothi, khusra, kojja, pavaiyaa etc. In society there is masculinities for men and feminities for women then what is wrong to accept both (masculinity and feminity) in intersex people? Why not include them as a gender in the society? Why not treat them equally as we treat each other? Why not make them feel at home in this society? Are we not responsible for their untold misery? Are they not "God Gifted" person who want to enjoy in this beautiful world? Is society is meant only for male and female? By not accepting them as normal human being are we not doing a crime? If 'no' think again and if 'yes' please stop.

Give them chance to grow up with us without any unwanted surgery. Give them all the rights to which they are entitled.

Hope this humble effort results in, growing even a single intersex child in the entire country in a friendly environment as a male and female child grows, I would consider my effort to have been worthwhile.

REFERENCE

1. Eugenides Jeffrey (2002). Middlesex, New York: Farras, Straus and Giroux.

Bibliography

Books

Agrawal, Anuja. (1997) "Gendered Bodies: The Case of the 'Third Gender' in India". In *Contributions to Indian Sociology*, new series, 31 273-97.

Ahmed, Mona and Dayanita Singh (photographer). (2001) Myself Mona Ahmed. Scalo Publishers, 15 September.

Artola, George T. (1975) "The Transvestite In Sanskrit Story and Dharma." *Annals of Oriental Research*, 57-68.

Basham, A.L. (1954) *The Wonder That Was India*. New York: Grove Press Inc.

Bedi, Rahula. (1994) "The Bizarre and Dangerous World of India's Eunuchs." *Vancouver Sun* (April 16, B1).

Bolin, Anne. (1988) *In Search of Eve: Transsexual Rites of Passage*. Massachusetts: Bergin and Garvey Publishers, Inc..

Brett Beemyn & Mickey Eliason, (1996) (editors), *Queer Studies: A Lesbian, Gay, Bisexual, & Transgender Anthology*, New York: New York University Press.

Burke, P. (1997). *Gender Shock: Exploring the Myths of Male and Female*. New York, NY: Anchor Books.

Butler, J. (1990). *Gender Trouble: Feminism and the Subversion of Identity*. New York, NY: Routledge.

Butler, J. (1993). *Bodies that matter: On the Discursive Limits of Sex*. New York, NY: Routledge.

Butler, J. (2004). *Undoing Gender*. New York, NY: Routledge.

Byne, William, *Scientific American: The Biological Evidence Challenged*, ebook.

Carstairs, George Morrison. (1956) "Hinjra and Jiryan: Two Derivatives of Hindu Attitudes to Sexuality." *British Journal of Medical Psychology* 29: 128-138.

Chandra, Abhik Kumar. (2000) "India's Reviled Eunuchs Take to The Election Soapbox." Agence France-Presse (February 16.

Chase, C. (2002) *Affronting Reason. GenderQueer: Voices From Beyond the Sexual Binary*. J. Nestle, C. Howell and R. Wilchins. Los Angeles, Alyson Books.

Cohen, Lawrence. (1995) "The Pleasures of Castration: The Postoperative Status of Hijras, Jankhas and Academics." In *Sexual Nature, Sexual Culture,*Paul R. Abramson and Steven D. Pinkerton, 276-304. Chicago: University of Chicago Press.

Colapinto, J. (2000). *As nature made him: The Boy Who was Raised as a Girl*. New York, NY: HarperCollins.

Coomaraswamy, Ananda K. and Sister Nivita. (1967) *Myths of the Hindus and Buddhists*. New York: Dover Publications Inc.

Coventry, M., (2000). The Tyranny of the esthetic: Surgery's most intimate violation. In: Disch, E. (ed.) *Reconstructing gender: A multicultural anthology* (2d edition) Second ed. Mountain View, California: Mayfield Publishing, 183-191.

Crawford, M., and Unger, R.K., (2000). *Women and gender: A feminist psychology*. 3rd (ed.) New York: McGraw Hill.

Devor, Holly (1997) FTM: *Female-to-male transsexuals in society*. Indiana University Press.

Diamond, M. and H.G. Beh (2006). The right to be wrong: Sex and gender decisions. In S. Sytsma (ed.), *Ethics & Intersex*. Dordrecht, NE: Springer.

Dreger, A (1999). *Intersex in the age of ethics*. Frederick Maryland: University Publishing Group.

Dreger, A. (1998). *Hermaphrodites and the Medical Invention of Sex*. Cambridge: Harvard University Press.

Dreger, Alice, (ed.) (1999) *Intersex in the Age of Ethics*. University Publishing Group.

Fausto-Sterling, A. (1992). *Myths of gender*. (2nd Ed.). New York: Basic Books.

Fausto-Sterling, A. (2000). *Sexing the body: Gender politics and the construction of sexuality*. New York: Basic Books.

Fausto-Sterling, A. (2005). *Bare bones of sex*: Part I, sex & gender. Signs, 30(2): 1491-528.

Fausto-Sterling, Anne (2000) *Sexing the Body: Gender Politics and the Construction of Sexuality*. Basic Books.

Feinberg, Leslie (1996) *Transgender warriors : making history from Joan of Arc to RuPaul*. Beacon Press

Feinberg, Leslie (1998) *Trans liberation: beyond pink or blue*. Beacon Press.

Goodman, A.; Heath, D.; Lindee, M.S. (eds) (2003) *Genetic Nature/Culture: Anthropology and Science beyond the Two-Culture Divide*. University of California Press.

Foucault, M. (1988). *The History of Sexuality*, vol.3: The care of the self. New York: Random House Inc.

Foucault, M. (1990). *The History of Sexuality*, vol.1: An introduction. New York: Random House Inc.

Freeman, James. *Untouchable: An Indian Life History*. Stanford: Stanford University Press. 1979.

Gannon, Shane Patrick. (2009) Translating the hijra: The symbolic reconstruction of the British Empire in India. PhD Thesis. University of Alberta.

Goldman, Robert P. (1993) "Transsexualism, Gender, and Anxiety in Traditional India." *Journal of the American Oriental Society* 113, no.3 (July – Sept., 374- 401.

Gordene Olga MacKenzie, (1994) Transgender Nation, Bowling Green, OH: Bowling Green University Popular Press.

Haber, Daniel B. (1997) "The Men Who Would Be Drag Queens." Inter Press Service (March 28.

Hall, Kira. (1997) "'Go Suck Your Husbands Sugarcane!': Hijras and the Use of Sexual Insult." In Anna Livia and Kira (ed) *Queerly Phrased: Language, Gender, and Sexuality*, Hall, Oxford: Oxford University Press.

Hampson, J.L., and J. G. Hampson (1961). *The ontogenesis of sexual behavior in man.* In W.C. Young (ed.), *Sex and Internal Secretions* (1401-1432), 3rd ed. Baltimore: Williams & Wilkins.

Hausman, Bernice (1995) *Changing Sex*: transsexualism, technology, and the idea of gender. Duke University Press.

Herdt, Gilbert, ed. (1994) *Third Sex, Third Gender: Beyond Sexual Dimorphism in Culture and History*. New York: Zone Books.

Hilfebeutel, Alf. (1980) "Siva, The Goddess, and The Disguises of The Pandavas and Draupadi." *History of Religions* 20 n.1-2 : 147-174.

Holmes, M. (2008). *Intersex: A Perilous Difference*. Selinsgrove, PA: Susquehanna University Press.

Holmes, M. (2009). *Critical Intersex*. Surrey, UK: Ashgate Press.

Jaffrey, Zia. (1996) *The Invisibles: A Tale of The Eunuchs of India*. New York: Vintage Books, Random House Inc.

Jami, Humaira. (2005) *Condition and Status of Hijras* (Transgender, Transvestites etc.) in Pakistan, National Institute of Psychology, Quaid-i-Azam University (nd)

John Colapinto, (2000) *As Nature Made Him: The Boy Who Was Raised as a Girl*, New York: HarperCollins.

John Money, (1991) *Biographies of Gender and Hermaphroditism in Paired Comparisons: Clinical Supplement to the Handbook of Sexology*, Amsterdam, Netherlands: Elsevier.

John Money, (1994) *Sex Errors of the Body and Related Syndromes: A Guide to Counseling Children, Adolescents, and Their Families*, Baltimore, MD: Paul H. Brooks Publishing Company, 2nd edition (ISBN: 1-55766-150-2;).

John Money, (1993) *The Adam Principle: Genes, Genitals, Hormones, & Gender: Selected Readings in Sexology*, Buffalo, NY: Prometheus Books.

Kessler, S. (1998). *Lessons from the intersexed*. New Brunswick, New Jersey: Rutgers University Press.

Kessler, S. and McKenna, W. (1978). *Gender: An ethnomethodological approach*. New York: John Wiley & Sons.

Maarriott, McKim. (1966) "The Feast of Love" In Milton Singer, (ed) *Krishna: Myths, Rites and Attitudes*, 200-212. Chicago: University of Chicago Press.

Mackay, Judith. (2000) *The Penguin Atlas of Human Sexual Behavior*. New York: Penguin Putnam Inc.

Malloy, Ruth Lor, (1997) *Meen Balaji and others. Hijras: Who We Are*. Toronto: Think Asia.

Mazur, T., Colsman, M., and Sandberg, D. E. (2007). Intersex: Definition, examples, gender stability, and the case against merging with transsexualism, In: Ettner, R., Monstrey, S., and Eyler, A. E. (eds). *Principles of Transgender Medicine and Surgery*. Binghamton: New York: Haworth Press, Inc.

Mccullough, L. B. (2002). A framework for the ethically justified clinical management of intersex conditions. In: Zderic, S. A. (ed). *Pediatric Gender Assignment: A Critical Reappraisal*. Kluwer Academic/Plenum Publishers, 149-173.

McGirk, Jan. (1998) "Street Life: Delhi- The Boy Who Ran Away to Join the Eunuchs." *The Independent* (October 20) 14.

Meyerowitz, J. (2002). *How sex changed: A history of transsexuality in the united states*. San Francisco, CA: Havard University Press.

Morris, G. (2003) Is it a boy or a girl? Portland.

Murray, Stephen O., and Roscoe, Will (1997). Islamic Homosexualities: Culture, History, and Literature. New York: New York University Press.

Nanda, S. (1999). *Gender diversity: Cross-cultural variations*. Illinoise, USA; Waveland Press.

Nanda, Serena. Neither Man nor Woman: The Hijras of India. Belmont: Wadsworth Publishing Company, 1999.

O"Flaherty, Wendy Doniger. Women, Androgynes, and Other Mythical Beasts. Chicago: University of Chicago Press, 1980.

Oostvogels, Robert (1995). *The Waria of Indonesia: A Traditional Third Gender Role*, in Herdt (ed.), *op cit.*

Opler, Morris E. "The Hijara (Hermaphrodites) of India and Indian National Character: A Rejoinder." *American Anthropologist 62* (1960): 505-511.

Parens, E. (2006). Surgically shaping children: Technology, ethics, and the pursuit of normality. Baltimore: Johns Hopkins University Press.

Pat Califia, (1994) *Public Sex: The Culture of Radical Sex*, San Francisco, CA: Cleis Press.

Patel, Geeta. (1997) "Home, Homo, Hybrid: Translating Gender." *College Literature* 24, 133-50.

Plant, R. (1986). The pink triangle: The Nazi war against homosexuals. New York: New Republic Books/Henry Hold and Company, Inc.

Preves, Sharon (2003) Intersex and Identity: The Contested Self, Rutgers University Press.

Ramet, S.P. (1996). *Gender reversals and gender cultures: Anthropological and historical perspectives*. New York, NY: Routledge.

Reis, E. (2000). American sexual histories: Blackwell readers in American social and cultural history. Malden, MA: Blackwell Publishers Inc.

Reyk, Nicola. "Feature: Hijras-India's 'Third Sex' Trigger Fear and Fascination" *Deutsche Press-Agentur* (September 5, 2000).

Robert J. Stoller, MD , Perversion: The Erotic Form of Hatred, New York: Pantheon, 1975, (reprint: London, UK: Karnac Books, 1986)

Robert J. Stoller, MD, (1985) *Presentations of Gender*, New Haven, CT: Yale UP.

Robert J. Stoller, MD, (1968) *Sex and Gender: On the Development of Masculinity and Femininity*, New York: Science House.

Roscoe, W. (1991). The zuni man-woman. Albuquerque: University of New Mexico Press.

Roscoe, W. (2000). Changing ones: Third and fourth genders in native north America.New York: Palgrave MacMillan.

Rosemary Joyce. (2000). *Gender and Power in Prehispanic Mesosamerica*. University of Texas Press.

Roughgarden, J.(2004). *Evolutions rainbow: Diversity, gender, and sexuality in nature and people*. California: University of California Press.

Schulte, J. (2004). *Paediatric and adolescent gynaecology: A multidisciplinary approach*. Balen, A.H. (ed). Cambridge University Press.

Sen, Amartya (2008). *AIDS Sutra: Untold Stories from India*. Anchor.

Shah, A.M. (1961) "A Note on the Hijadas of Gujarat." *American Anthropologist* 61, 1325-1220.

Sharma, Satish Kumar. "Eunuchs: Past and Present." *The Eastern Anthropologist* 37, no.4 (1984): 381-389.

Stein, Edward (1999) *The mismeasure of desire: the science, theory and ethics of sexual orientation*. Oxford University Press.

Suzanne J. Kessler, (1998) Lessons from the Intersexed, New Brunswick, NJ: Rutgers University Press.

Sweet, Michael J. and Leonard Zwilling. "The First Medicalization: The Taxonomy and Etiology of Queerness in Classical Indian Medicine." *Journal of the History of Sexuality* 3, no.4 (1993) 590-607.

Sytsma, Sharon, ed. (2006) *Ethics and Intersex*. Springer.

Szuchman, L.T. and Muscarella, F. (1999). *Psychological perspectives on human sexuality*. Denny, D. (ed). Danvers: Wiley.

Talwar, Rajesh. (1999) *The Third Sex and Human Rights*. Gyan Publishing House,

Turner, S. (1999). Intersex Identities: Locating New Intersections of Sex and Gender. *Gender & Society,* 13(4): 457-479.

Varam, Dev. (1997) "Indian Eunuchs Seek Sympathy Through Book." *Reuters* (February 14).

Wiederman, M., (2001). Transgenderism on video (includes reviews of hermaphrodites speak! And xxxy). *Journal of Sex Research*, 38 (2), 175-178.

Wilhelm, Amara Das (2004). Tritiya Prakriti (People of the Third Sex): *Understanding Homosexuality, Transgender Identity and Intersex Conditions through Hinduism* (XLibris Corporation.

Wilson, B. E., and Reiner, W. G., 1999. Management of intersex: A shifting paradigm. In: Dreger, A. D. ed. *Intersex in the age of ethics*. Hagerstown, Maryland: University Publishing Group, 119-136.

Zderic, S.A., Canning, D.A., Carr, M.C., and Snyder, H.M. (Eds.). (2002). *Pediatric assignment of sex: A critical reappraisal*. New York: Kluwer Academic/Plenum.

Articles

Alibadi SA. (2004) "Gender assignment surgery for intersexed infants: How the substantive due process right to privacy both supports and opposes a moratorium." 12 *Virginia Journal of Social Policy & the Law* 170.

Alibadi SA. (2005)"You make me feel like a natural woman: Allowing parents to consent to early gender assignment surgeries for their intersexed infants." *William and Mary Journal of Women and the Law* 427. 2005

American Academy of Pediatrics Section on Endocrinology and Section on Urology Committee on Genetics. (2000). Evaluation of the newborn with developmental anomalies of the external genitalia. *Pediatrics*, 106 (01), 138-142. Available from: http://aappolicy.aappublications.org/cgi/content/full/pediatrics;106/1/138.

American Academy of Pediatrics Section on Urology. (1996). Timing of elective surgery on the genitalia of male children with particular reference to the risks, benefits, and psychological effects of surgery and anesthesia. *Pediatrics*, 97 (4), 590-594. Available from: http://aappolicy.aappublications.org/cgi/reprint/pediatrics;97/4/590.pdf.

Beh HG, Diamond M. (2000). "An emerging ethical and medical dilemma: Should physicians perform sex assignment on infants with ambiguous genitalia?" *Michigan Journal of Gender & Law*, 7(1): 1-63.

Beh HG, Diamond M. (2005). "David Reimer's legacy: Limiting parental discretion." 12 *Cardozo Journal of Law & Gender* 5.

Ben-Asher N. (2005). "The necessity of sex change: A struggle for intersex and trans liberties." 29 *Harvard Journal of Law & Gender* 51.

Benson , S.R. (2005). Hacking the gender binary myth: Recognizing fundamental rights for the intersexed. *Cardozo Journal of Law & Gender*, 12.

Benson SR. (2005). "Hacking the gender binary myth: recognizing fundamental rights for the intersexed." 12 *Cardozo Journal of Law & Gender* 31.

Bird J. (2005). "Outside the law: Intersex, medicine, and the discourse of rights." 12 Cardozo *Journal of Law & Gender 65.*

Bishop EA. (2007). "A child's expertise: Establishing statutory protection for intersexed children who reject their gender of assignment." 82 *New York University Law Review.*

Blackless, M., Charuvastra, A., Derryck, A., Fausto-Sterling, A., & Lauzanne, K., Lee, K. (2000). How sexually dimorphic are we? Review and synthesis. *American Journal of Human Biology*, (12): 151-166.

Bloom A. (2005(. "Rupture, leakage, and reconstruction: The body as a site for the enforcement and reproduction of sex-based legal norms in the breast implant controversy." *Columbia Journal of Gender & Law* 85.

Bolton, Jessica (2009). An Examination of Transgender Youth: Support Networks and Mental Health Concerns. PhD. Dissertation, *School of Professional Psychology*, Pacific University..

Braren, V., Slonim, A., Warner, J. J., O'neill, J. A., Jr., Burr, I. M., and Rhamy, R. K., (1980). True hermaphroditism: A rational appraoch to diagnosis and treatment. Urology, 15 (6), 569-574. Available from: http://www.ncbi.nlm.nih.gov/htbin-post/Entrez/query? db=m&form= 6&dopt=r&uid= 7394982.

British Association of Paediatric Surgeons Working Party on the Surgical Management of Children Born with Ambiguous Genitalia. 2001. Statement of the british association of paediatric surgeons working party on the surgical management of children born with ambiguous genitalia. Available from: http://www.baps. org.uk/ documents/ Intersex %20statement.htm

Broeck, Shannon R (2005). Categories of Gender & Sexuality: Exploring the Relationship between Language and the Formation of Non-Heteronormative Identities. Honors Thesis, University of California, San Diego.

CBC News (2002). Medical first: a uterus transplant. [Web]. Retrieved from http:// www.cbsnews. com /stories/2002/03/07/health/main503195.shtml

Claman, Erica Elaine (2007). An Examination of the Predictors of Attitudes Toward Transgender Individuals. PhD. Dissertation, *Psychology*, The Ohio State University.

Cote A. (2000). "Telling the truth? Disclosure, therapeutic privilege and intersexuality in children." *Health Law Journal* 8:199-216.

Coventry, M., (1998). Summer. The tyranny of the esthetic: Surgery's most intimate violation. On the Issues: The Progressive Woman's Quarterly, 7, 16-23,60-61. Available from: http://mosaic.echonyc.com/~onissues/su98coventry.html

Crisovan, Piper Lauren (2006). "Risky" business: Cultural conceptions of HIV/AIDS in Indonesia. PhD. Dissertation, Anthropology, University of Pittsburgh.

Dewing, P., Shi, T., Horvath, S., & Vilain, E. (2003). Sexually dimorphic gene expression in mouse brain precedes gonadal differentiation. *Journal of Molecular Brain Research*, 118(1/2).

Diamond M, Sigmundson HK (1997). Sex reassignment at birth: A long term review and clinical Implications. Archives of Pediatrics and Adolescent Medicine, 151: 298-304.

Diamond, M. (1965). A critical evaluation of the ontology of human sexual behavior. The Quarterly Review of Biology, 40(2). [Web]. Retrieved from http://www.hawaii.edu/ PCSS/ online_artcls/intersex/qrb_201.html

Dreger AD. (2001) "Ambiguous sex'—or ambivalent medicine? Ethical problems in treatment of intersexuality." Women, Medicine and Law. S Sherwin. London: Ashgate Publishing.

Eckert, Christina Annalena (2003). The Historicisation of the Hermaphroditic/Intersexed Body: From Medicalisation to De-Medicalisation. Master's Dissertation, *Gender History*, University of Essex.

Ehrenreich N, Barr M. (2005). "Intersex surgery, female genital cutting, and the selective condemnation of 'cultural practices'." Harvard Civil Rights-Civil Liberties Law Review, Winter; 40(1):71-140.

Escobar, Laura Maria (2008). Progressive care : an examination of male to female transgender sex workers' experiences within the health care and social service systems in San Francisco, California. MSW Dissertation, Smith College School for Social Work, Northampton, Mass..

Evans, Richard Neil (2009). A Philosophical Exploration of Transsexuality. PhD Dissertation, The University of Birmingham.

Fawcett, Fred (1891). On Basivis: Women Who, through Dedication to a Deity, Assume Masculine Privileges. *Journal of the Anthropological Society of Bombay* (July). Bombay: Education Society's Press; London: Treubner.

Ford K-K. (2001). "'First, do no harm': The fiction of legal parental consent to genital-normalizing surgery on intersexed infants." Yale Law & Policy Review.

Fox M, Thomson M. (2005). "Cutting it: Surgical interventions and the sexing of children." 12 *Cardozo Journal of Law & Gender* 81.

Frankle RE. (2003). "Does a marriage really need sex?: A critical analysis of the gender restriction on marriage." *Fordham Urban Law Journal September*.

Gallacher L (2003). The psychology of intersex: Research into the experiences of individuals who have experienced abdrogen insensity syndrome or congenital adrenal hyperplasia within the UK. M.A. Thesis. University of York.

Genel, Myron. (2000). Gender verification no more?. Medscape Women's Health, 5(3), Retrieved from http://ai.eecs.umich.edu/people/conway/TS/OlympicGenderTesting.html

Germon, Jennifer E (2006). Generations of gender: past, present, potential. PhD. Dissertation, University of Sydney.

Greatheart, Marcus Skidley (2010). The Fred Study: stories of life satisfaction and wellness from post-transition transgender men. Master's Dissertation, Social Work, University of British Columbia..

Greenberg JA. (1999). "Defining male and female: Intersexuality and the collision between law and biology." *Arizona Law Review* 41(2):265-328.

Greenberg JA. (2005). "Intersex and intersex debates: Building alliances to challenge sex discrimination." 12 *Cardozo Journal of Law & Gender* 99.

Greenwood Swanson, Hunter (2009). Standards of Care: Transgender/Genderqueer Clients' Experiences with Mental Health Workers. Master's Dissertation, Smith College School for Social Work, Northampton, Massachusetts..

Grey, Leslee (2009). Multiple Selves, Fractured (Un)learnings: The Pedagogical Significance of Drag Kings' Narratives. PhD. Dissertation, Educational Policy Studies, Department of Educational Policy Studies, College of Education, Georgia State University.

Guber N. (2005). "Ethics in medicine: With a special focus on the concepts of sex and gender in intersex management." 12 *Cardozo Journal of Law & Gender* 117.

Haas K. (2004). "Who will make room for the intersexed?" *Americal Journal of Law and Medicine 30*(1):41-68.

Hermer L. (2002). "Paradigms revised: Intersex children, bioethics & the law." Annals of Health Law.

Hermer L. (2007). "A moratorium on inersex surgeries? Law, Science, Identity, and bioethics at the crossroads." *Cardozo Journal of Law & Gender*.

Hill, Robert S (2007). 'As a man I exist; as a woman I live': Heterosexual Transvestism and the Contours of Gender and Sexuality in Postwar America. PhD. Dissertation, University of Michigan.

Hird, Myra. (2003). Considerations for a psycho-analytic theory of gender identity and sexual desire: the case of intersex. Signs: Journal of Women in Culture and Society, 28(4), Retrieved from http://www.queensu.ca/sociology/files/Considerations% 20for%20a% 20Psychoanalytic%20 Theory.pdf

Holmes M. (2005). "Distracted attentions: Intersexuality and human rights protections." *Cardozo Journal of Law & Gender* 127.

Holmes, M. (2008). Distracted attentions: Intersexuality and human rights protection. *Cardozo Journal of Gender and the Law*, 12, 127-133.

Holmes, M. (2008). Mind the gaps: Intersex and (re)productive spaces in disability studies and bioethics. *Journal of Bioethical Inquiry*, 5(2/3).

Johnson, Christine (2004). Transsexualism: An Unacknowledged Endpoint Of Developmental Endocrine Disruption? Master's dissertation, *Environmental Studies*, Evergreen State College..

Kalterborn B (2003). The Fa'afafine, gender benders in Samoa: On cultural construction of gender and role change. PhD Dissertation, University of Oslo..

Kenagy GP (1998). Exploring an Oppressed Group: A Study of the Health and Social Service Needs of Transgendered People in Philadelphia. Ph.D Dissertation. University of Pennsylvania.

Knouse J. (2005). "Intersexuality and the social construction of anatomical sex." *Cardozo Journal of Law & Gender* 135.

Kruijver, P.M., Zhou, J., Pool, C.W., Hofman, M.A., Gooren, L.J.G., and Swaab, D.F. (2000). Male-to-female transsexuals have female neuron numbers in a limbic nucleus". *Journal of Clinical Endocrinology and Metabolism*, 85(5), 2034:2041.

Kurtz SF. (2000). "The law of informed consent: From 'doctor is right' to 'patient has rights'." *Syracuse Law Review*.

Lair, Liam Oliver (2009). Beyond whiteness and ideal masculinity; expanding transgendered identity. Master's Dissertation, Roosevelt University.

Lareau AC. (2003). "Who decides? Genital normalizing surgery on intersexed infants." *Georgetown Law Journal*. 92.

Leslie JA, Cain MP, Rink RC. (2009). Feminizing genital reconstruction in congenital adrenal hyperplasia. *Indian Journal of Urology,* 25:17-26.

Levi J. (2006). "The interplay between disability and sexuality: Clothes don't make the man (or woman), but gender identity might." *Columbia Journal of Gender & Law* 15: 90.

Lloyd E. (2005). Symposium report: Intersex education, advocacy, & the law: The struggle for recognition and protection. *Cardozo Women's Law Journal,* 11.

Lloyd E. (2005). "From the hospital to the courtroom: A statutory proposal for recognizing and protecting the legal rights of intersex children." 12 *Cardozo Journal of Law & Gender* 155.

Lloyd E. (2005). "Symposium report: Intersex education, advocacy, & the law: The struggle for recognition and protection." *Cardozo Women's Law Journal* 283

Lloyd, J., Crouch, N.S., Minto, C.L., Liao, L., & Ceighton, S.M. (2005). Female genital appearance: 'Normality unfolds'. *International Journal of Obstetrics and Gynecology,* 112: 643-46.

Loehr K (2007). Transvestites in Buenos Aires: Prostitution, Poverty & Policy. Master's Dissertation, Georgetown University & Universidad de San Martin.

MacDonald, Danielle (2009). Photography as Therapy in the Transgender Community. Senior Thesis, University of Maine, Farmington..

Martin PL. (2002). "Moving toward an international standard in informed consent: The impact of intersexuality and the internet on the standard of care." *Duke Journal of Gender Law & Policy Summer.*

Matza, Alexis (2009). The Boston "T" Party: Masculinity, Testosterone Therapy, And Embodiment Among Aging Men And Transgender Men. PhD. Dissertation, *Anthropology,* The University of Iowa.

McNichols WJ (1995). "Informed consent liability in a 'material information' jurisdiction: What does the future portend?" *Oklahoma Law Review*.

Meredith, Leah (2000). The meaning of lived experience of transexual individuals. Master's Dissertation, University of British Columbia..

Morland ICF (2005). Narrating Intersex: On the ethical critique of the medical management of intersexuality, 1985-2005. PHD Thesis. Royal Holloway, University of London.

Morland, I. (2009). What can queer theory do for intersex? *A Journal of Lesbian and Gay Studies* (15):2, 285-312.

Pfeffer. Carla A (2009). Trans(Formative) Relationships: What We Learn About Identities, Bodies, Work and Families from Women Partners of Trans Men. PhD. Dissertation, *Sociology*, University of Michigan.

Pimplay, P.N. and S.K. Sharma (1985). "Hijaras: A Study of an Atypical Role." *Avadh Journal of Social Sciences* 2 42-50.

Preston, Laurence W. (1987) "A Right to Exist: Eunuchs and the State in Nineteen- Century India." Modern Asian Studies 21 no.2 371-387.

Preves S. (2005). "Out of the O.R. and into the streets: Exploring the impact of intersex media activism." *Cardozo Journal of Law & Gender* 12: 247.

Reilly E. (2005). "Radical tweak—Relocating the power to assign sex: From enforcer of differentiation to facilitator of inclusiveness: Revising the response to intersexuality." *Cardozo Journal of Law & Gender* 12: 297.

Ritchie, Laura Renee (2008). Disclosure of Sexual Orientation by Adult Children to Their Family-of-Origin: Effects Upon quality of Family Relationship. PhD Dissertation, University of North Carolina at Charlotte..

Rosato JL. (2000). "Using bioethics discourse to determine when parents should make health care decisions for their minor children: Is deference justified?" *Temple Law Review*, Spring 2000.

Ryan, Joelle Ruby (2009). Reel Gender: Examining the Politics of Trans Images in Film and Media. PhD. Dissertation, American Culture Studies/Popular Culture, Bowling Green State University..

Saunders, Karen (2008). Queer intercorporeality: Body Disruption of Straight Space. Master's Dissertation, Gender Studies, University of Canterbury, Christchurch, Aotearoa/ New Zealand..

Saunders, Sean (2007). Crossing out: transgender (in)visibility in twentieth-century culture. PhD. Dissertation, University of British Columbia.

Schmidt, Johanna Mary (2005). Migrating Genders: Westernisation, migration, and Samoan fa'afafine. PhD, Dissertation, *Sociology*, The University of Auckland.

Stone MR. (2005). "Approaching critical mass: An exploration of the role of intersex allies in creating positive education, advocacy, and change." *Cardozo Journal of Law & Gender* 12: 353.

Svoboda JS, Van Howe RS, Dwyer JG. (2000). "Informed consent for neonatal circumcision: An ethical and legal conundrum." *Journal of Contemporary Health Law & Policy*. 17:61-133.

Waszkiewicz, Elroi (2006). Getting by Gatekeepers: Transmen's Dialectical Negotiations within Psychomedical Institutions. Master's Dissertation, *Sociology*, Georgia State University.

Wharton, Virginia Wyatt (2007). Gender variance and mental health : a national survey of transgender trauma history, posttraumatic stress, and disclosure in therapy. MSW Dissertation, Smith College School for Social Work, Northampton, Mass.

White, Caroline (2002). Re/Defining Gender and Sex: Educating for Trans, Transsexual, and Intersex Access and Inclusion to Sexual Assault Centres and Transition Houses. Master's Dissertation, Department of Educational Studies, University of British Columbia.

Wisniewski, A., (2001). Book review: Hermaphrodites and the medical invention of sex. *The Journal of Nervous and Mental Disease*, 189 (3), 197-198.

Woodhouse, C. R. J., (1994). The sexual and reproductive consequences of congenital genitourinary anomalies. *Journal of Urology*, 152 (August 1994), 645-651.

Woodhouse, C. R. J., (1997). Quality of life in children and adolescents: A urologist's point of view. *Dialogues in Pediatric Urology*, 20 (11), 7-8.

Woodman, S., (1996). March. Sexual healing? *Allure*, 120-122.

Wyatt Wharton, Virginia (2007). Gender Variance and Mental Health: A National Survey of Transgender Trauma History, Posttraumatic Stress, and Disclosure in Therapy. Master's Dissertation, Smith College School for Social Work, Northampton, Massachusetts.

Index